KU-449-738

Vegan & Gluten-Free
BAKING

Vegan & Gluten-Free BAKING

Over 80 delicious vegan and gluten-free recipes!

With foreword by The Vegan Society CEO

Jasmijn de Boo

This edition published by Parragon Books Ltd in 2014
LOVE FOOD is an imprint of Parragon Books Ltd

Parragon Books Ltd
Chartist House
15–17 Trim Street
Bath BA1 1HA, UK
www.parragon.com/lovefood

ISBN: 978-1-4723-4904-0

Printed in China

New recipes and introduction by Jane Hughes
Foreword by Jasmijn de Boo
New photography by Noel Murphy
Home economy by Penny Stephens
Cover and internal design by Geoff Borin

Notes for the reader
This book uses both metric and imperial measurements. Follow the same units of measurement throughout; do not mix metric and imperial. All spoon measurements are level: teaspoons are assumed to be 5 ml, and tablespoons are assumed to be 15 ml. Unless otherwise stated, individual vegetables are medium and pepper is freshly ground black pepper. Unless otherwise stated, all root vegetables should be peeled prior to using.

Garnishes, decorations and serving suggestions are all optional and not necessarily included in the recipe ingredients or method. The times given are an approximate guide only. Preparation times differ according to the techniques used by different people and the cooking times may also vary from those given. Optional ingredients, variations or serving suggestions have not been included in the time calculations.

Vegan and gluten-free diets
While the author has made all reasonable efforts to ensure that the information contained in this book is accurate and up to date at the time of publication, anyone reading this book should note the following important points:-

Medical and pharmaceutical knowledge is constantly changing and the author and the publisher cannot and do not guarantee the accuracy or appropriateness of the contents of this book;

In any event, this book is not intended to be, and should not be relied upon, as a substitute for appropriate, tailored professional advice. Both the author and the publisher strongly recommend that a doctor or other healthcare professional is consulted before embarking on major dietary changes;

For the reasons set out above, and to the fullest extent permitted by law, the author and publisher: (i) cannot and do not accept any legal duty of care or responsibility in relation to the accuracy or appropriateness of the contents of this book, even where expressed as 'advice' or using other words to this effect; and (ii) disclaim any liability, loss, damage or risk that may be claimed or incurred as a consequence – directly or indirectly – of the use and/or application of any of the contents of this book.

The publisher has been careful to select recipes that do not contain animal products or ingredients with gluten.
Any ready-made ingredients that could potentially contain animal products or gluten have been listed as 'vegan' and 'gluten-free' so readers know to look for the vegan or gluten-free versions. However, always read labels carefully and, if necessary, check with the manufacturer.

Contents

FOREWORD FROM THE VEGAN SOCIETY'S CEO,

JASMIJN DE BOO

I believe it was on the first birthday after I became vegan, just over 10 years ago, that I tried to make a cheesecake with silken tofu using a recipe that I found somewhere online. Unfortunately, some of my guests were not very impressed. I had either not stuck to the precise measurements or I might have substituted an ingredient for something that was not available. The result was edible, but not very appealing.

But it doesn't need to be this way! In the last 10 years, we have seen more and more vegan baking recipes being shared, loved and praised, including by thousands of non- or not-yet-vegans. Vegan and gluten-free diets are increasingly popular and, whatever your diet, we all share a common interest in wanting to cook, eat and share tasty and varied treats.

Whether you are cooking for yourself or for a friend or loved one, *Vegan & Gluten-Free Baking* will be a great addition to your cookery book shelf. The instructions couldn't be clearer, so no more tofu cheesecake disasters for me! For those with a sweet tooth there are plenty of ideas here, such as Chocolate Mint Marble Cake or Caramel Peach Bars. Fruit lovers are served well with recipes such as Apricot & Apple Spiced Loaf, Fig Upside-Down Cake, Orange & Cinnamon Muffins, and White Chocolate & Raspberry Tartlets. And I am sure that the interesting inclusion of savoury bakes, such as Cheese & Chive Bread, Beetroot Muffins and Herby Scones, will make this unique collection very popular.

I wholeheartedly recommend this book to you: the variety and flavours are the most inspiring I have seen in any vegan and gluten-free baking book to date.

Jasmijn de Boo

CEO, The Vegan Society
www.vegansociety.com

WHY EAT A VEGAN AND GLUTEN-FREE DIET?

Interest in both veganism and gluten-free food has rocketed over the past few years, for a variety of reasons, and an increasing number of people are looking for recipes that tick both boxes. Vegan food is acceptable to a very wide range of people and ensuring that the food you offer is also gluten-free means that almost everybody can enjoy it!

THE VEGAN DIET

Veganism is often seen as a logical next step for vegetarians, as many vegetarians feel uncomfortable about the industrial-scale farming increasingly involved with the production of milk and eggs. The vegan diet does not include any foods of animal origin and most vegans extend this principle to other aspects of their lifestyle, by avoiding clothing made from leather or wool, as well as toiletries, cosmetics and cleaning products that contain ingredients derived from animals or that have been tested on animals. As awareness of the vegan lifestyle increases, it is becoming easier to find products of all kinds that are suitable for this ethical choice.

Although most vegans opt for this lifestyle for ethical reasons, believing that a plant-based diet is better for the environment, better for their health and kinder to animals, there are some vegetarians who tend towards a vegan diet not through choice but because of food intolerances or allergies related to dairy products or eggs.

THE GLUTEN-FREE DIET

Most people who follow a strict gluten-free diet do so for medical reasons. For those with serious conditions, such as coeliac disease, eating gluten can cause a reaction that is both painful and dangerous. For this reason, it is essential that any food that is sold as gluten free is truly safe for those with serious allergies or intolerances. But there are a growing number of people who are experiencing milder intolerances to wheat and other foods that contain gluten. Many have found that they have trouble digesting these foods and have adjusted their diets accordingly.

Food intolerances vary widely, with some people finding that they can tolerate small amounts of gluten, or that spelt, an ancient variety of wheat, seems easier to digest. Over many centuries, the wheat that we grow has been modified by selective breeding to give it desirable characteristics, such as hardiness in the field, resistance to disease and a predictable pattern of growth and ripening. Some argue that modern wheat is now so far removed from the plants that used to flourish in the wild that it can barely be said to be a natural food and many people believe that this is the root of their dietary problems.

It is also true to say that the typical Western diet contains far more gluten than it used to – how many of us tuck in to toast or cereal for breakfast, biscuits at coffee time, sandwiches for lunch, and perhaps a slice of cake or a cereal bar in the afternoon before our main evening meal? If that main meal is a pie, a tart or a pasty, a stew with dumplings, a pancake or a flatbread, something cooked in or topped with breadcrumbs, or pasta or a pizza, then we may well have consumed gluten at every meal. We may not even realise that the food we are eating is made with wheat, as wheat products are widely used in all kinds of ready meals and may not be obvious, unless you check the list of ingredients on the pack. Over-consumption of any kind of food can tend to precipitate unwanted reactions as the body struggles to cope with an overload, and, in the long term, a sustained overload can lead to a sudden serious reaction or a permanent allergy.

VEGAN AND GLUTEN-FREE BAKING

Baking without gluten presents some challenges. Gluten-free pastry can be crumbly and, without gluten, breads and cakes may not rise well. Many gluten-free recipes tend to rely on eggs to overcome these problems but, of course, that is not an option for vegan bakers. This book contains tried-and-tested recipes developed using a variety of techniques and ingredients to make sure your vegan, gluten-free cakes and bakes are successful.

8lb
2kg

VEGAN AND GLUTEN-FREE BAKING TIPS

The first thing to do when you are aiming to bake vegan and gluten free is to make absolutely sure that you are using the right ingredients. There are stumbling blocks for unwary cooks who might assume that all margarines and all dark chocolates are suitable for vegans or that cooking without wheat is just the same as cooking without gluten.

It's also really important to check the equipment you are using. Experienced bakers may be in the habit of making substitutions, knowing that things will probably work out. But recipes without gluten and animal products can be less forgiving. So, here are some helpful tips:

- Use the right size of cake tin. Using a smaller tin could mean a thicker cake that will struggle to rise and a larger tin could mean your cake heats through too quickly and becomes rubbery.
- Follow the instructions about mixing ingredients. There may be very good reasons why the ingredients are combined in specific ways (see also the note on baking powder below). Some recipes really benefit from being beaten in an electric food processor, whereas others give the best result when they are just quickly stirred together.
- Follow the instructions about lining tins – mixtures that contain egg replacer and xanthan gum can be particularly difficult to remove from unlined tins and can also stick to lining paper as they cool.
- Follow the instructions about cooling your bakes. Some things need to be allowed to cool before they can be moved, otherwise they will break. Other things need to come out of the tins quickly, otherwise they will 'sweat' and become unpleasantly damp.

A NOTE ABOUT BAKING POWDER

Some standard commercial baking powders are not gluten free – make sure you buy a brand that is labelled gluten free. Baking powder is a dry mixture of a weak acidic powder (typically cream of tartar) and a weak alkaline powder (typically sodium bicarbonate). When liquid is added, the chemical reaction creates bubbles of carbon dioxide that will make your cake rise. In cake mixtures that contain eggs, the cake cooks around the bubbles to produce a sponge. In vegan, gluten-free cakes, the bubbles can rush to the surface of the cake and burst without providing the rising effect.

If your cake is not rising, it may be because you have left the mixture for too long before putting it in the oven. As soon as the wet and dry mixtures are combined and the baking powder starts to act, the cake should go into the oven. If there is any delay (while you spoon the mixture into a tin or divide it between cupcake cases), lift up the baking tin and rap it on your kitchen counter once or twice immediately before you put it into the oven – you will see some bubbles burst on the surface of the mixture. This simple tip will stop your cakes from rising too quickly and then collapsing before the cake mixture is firm.

A NOTE ABOUT OVEN TEMPERATURE

Oven temperature is critical and it's very useful to have an oven thermometer that will tell you what's really going on in there. Most ovens maintain a 'ballpark' temperature by switching the heat on and off, and in some cases this can result in a noticeable fluctuation in temperature. When you preheat your oven, it may indicate that it is ready to use long before the desired temperature is actually achieved. As a rule, vegan, gluten-free bakes should be placed on a shelf in the centre of the oven, not too high or too low. It's best not to rely on rotating cake tins between high and low shelves as you bake, because the rush of cool air that hits your cakes as you open the oven door can have catastrophic effects.

If you are baking a cake with several layers and you can't get all your tins onto the middle shelf at once, the best option is to make the cake in several batches. Cake mixture that is allowed to stand while you wait for oven space will quickly lose its ability to rise. This can make baking layer cakes rather time-consuming, but if you want each layer to rise properly and all the layers to be equal, it's better to be safe than sorry. The same applies if you want to make a lot of muffins or cupcakes – don't multiply the ingredients up and then leave half the mixture to sit in a bowl while you bake the first batch of cakes, instead make two or three separate batches of cake mix.

HOW TO BAKE VEGAN

Many vegans enjoy cooking and like to make their food from scratch, partly so that they know exactly what they are eating and partly because they prefer to eat plant-based foods that are fresh and not treated with any flavour enhancers or preservatives.

Many recipes are easy to 'veganize' but baking is a science and attempting to customize recipes can lead to some unexpected results.

REPLACEMENTS FOR BUTTER

Many people prefer to use margarine instead of butter in cooking and making this switch seems straightforward. It is important to realize that not all margarines are suitable for vegans – many still contain dairy products and some are fortified with vitamins that are derived from non-vegan sources. Some low-fat spreads contain gelatine and non-vegan lecithin, which are both added to improve their texture.

There are all sorts of vegan margarines and butter substitutes available and new products are being developed all the time. Products vary, but margarines may contain more water than fat and this can have adverse effects when it is used for baking. Some people who are vegan for health reasons are also concerned that margarine is not a 'natural' product and often contains unhealthy trans fats. For these reasons, many vegan recipes use light vegetables oils such as rapeseed oil or coconut oil.

REPLACEMENTS FOR MILK

Soya milk was the first vegan milk replacement to be widely commercially available, but the market is expanding rapidly, with milks made from almonds, rice, oats, coconuts and hazelnuts all becoming popular. Vegan milks of all kinds tend to contain less fat and more water than dairy milk and this can affect results when baking. Soya milk has a particular tendency to curdle when vinegar or lemon juice is added and, although this looks rather unpleasant, the result is a useful substitute for buttermilk in vegan baking.

All kinds of vegan creams and yogurts are now being developed, many based on soya or coconut milk. These can work well when served with vegan puddings and cakes, but results can be unpredictable when they are used in baking, with some products splitting and becoming watery. Coconut cream is satisfyingly creamy but high in saturated fats, making it more suitable for occasional treats than everyday use.

REPLACEMENTS FOR EGGS

Eggs have interesting properties when it comes to baking – they can help cakes rise, hold dough together, add a glaze, make a sponge springy or a cracker crisp. There are a number of ways to replace eggs in vegan baking and the best choice depends upon the result you are looking for. Some vegan muffin recipes use applesauce to add body and moisture to a recipe. Others may use ground linseeds, which have a gelatinous consistency when mixed with water and can help create a spongy texture. Both of these ingredients are most successful in muffins, which tend to have a denser and chewier texture than sponge cakes. Commercial egg replacement powders can often help to make biscuits crisp, give a lift to sponges and can even be used to make vegan meringue-style toppings for pies. For glazing, soya milk or a mixture of soya flour and water can produce good results.

OTHER VEGAN SUBSTITUTIONS

Vegan bakers need to take care with some other ingredients, too. Dark chocolate is not necessarily vegan and, although there are good varieties of vegan chocolate available (including substitutes for milk and white chocolate), these may behave unpredictably when heated, separating into an oil mixture or hardening into lumps. It's important to note that some brands of icing sugar are made with dried egg, some cake sprinkles contain gelatine and some food colourings are not suitable for vegans, notably cochineal (E120) as this is derived from insects. Beetroot powder is a natural food colouring that produces a vibrant pink or red colour, which is perfect for making icing but tends to turn brown when baked in cakes that contain baking powder. Try decorating cakes with shavings of vegan chocolate, crystallized fruit, or sugar mixed with vegan-friendly food colourings.

Fruit can sometimes be given a wax coating that is made from animal products so be careful to select unwaxed fruit. Sugar can also be produced using animal bones, so check the packaging to ensure it is vegan.

HOW TO BAKE GLUTEN FREE

Finding gluten-free food is becoming easier all the time and substitutions are generally quite straightforward. However, baking without gluten can be tricky, especially if you are not using eggs. Many gluten-free baking recipes rely on the use of eggs to help bind mixtures and provide the elasticity that makes dough easier to work, and baked goods more likely to rise.

Anybody with a serious intolerance or allergy to gluten will be well aware of which foods are off limits, but for other people, it might not be so obvious. Wheat, spelt, rye and barley all contain gluten and oats contain a gluten-like protein which many coeliac sufferers prefer to avoid. Semolina and couscous also contain gluten as they are made with wheat. Some baking powder is not gluten free and you will need to make sure you check the label says gluten free. It's also important to realise that wheat free doesn't necessarily mean gluten free.

GLUTEN-FREE FLOURS AND STARCHES

- **Amaranth** – best used as part of a gluten-free flour mix, this can improve the texture of a gluten-free bake and also adds to the nutritional value. It has a pleasant peppery flavour.
- **Arrowroot** – a ground plant root that is used rather like cornflour as a thickener.
- **Brown and white rice flour** – brown rice flour is heavier and more nutritious than white. Best used in combination with other gluten-free flours.
- **Buckwheat** – this is not wheat and does not contain gluten. It has a strong, bitter flavour that works well in breads and pancakes.
- **Coconut flour** – finely milled dried coconut, which is tasty but can be dense and dry. Best used as part of a mixture of gluten-free flours.
- **Gram flour** – ground chickpeas, often used in Indian and Italian breads and baking.
- **Millet flour** – a powdery yellow flour with a sweet flavour that works well in muffins and sweet breads.
- **Polenta/cornmeal** – used in cakes and breads to help retain moisture, it also adds colour, texture and flavour to bakes.
- **Potato flour** – a heavy flour with a strong flavour best used sparingly. Potato starch is a different product, which does not have a strong flavour and can add moisture and a soft texture to baked goods.
- **Quinoa flour** – rich in protein with a pleasant nutty taste, this works well in cakes, cookies and breads.
- **Sorghum flour** – this has a sweet, nutty flavour and works best with other gluten-free flours.
- **Soya flour** – used mainly as a thickener, this adds a nutty flavour and a light texture to a mixture of gluten-free flours.
- **Tapioca flour** – a starch extracted from the cassava root, native to South America. It has a sweet taste and adds texture to a mixture of gluten-free flours.
- **Teff flour** – made from a nutritious grain native to Africa, this has a flavour that has been likened to hazelnuts.

Finely ground nuts, such as almonds, hazelnuts, chestnuts, pecans and walnuts, and seeds, such as linseeds, hemp and chia, can also be used in conjunction with gluten-free flours to change the flavour or texture of a bake.

Each gluten-free flour has its own properties – some are tasty but heavy, others light but bland – and for this reason the most successful gluten-free bakes tend to be made with mixtures of different flours. It is quite straightforward to find these gluten-free flour blends in supermarkets and health food stores and the blends have been developed to create flours that give good results across a variety of recipes. However, if you do a lot of gluten-free baking, you might enjoy experimenting with your own blends and you might find that this saves you money too.

Once you have your gluten-free flour blend, don't assume that you can use it in any standard baking recipe. Pastry made with gluten-free flour can be too crumbly to use, yeasted breads do not rise well, and cakes made with baking powder may rise too quickly and then deflate before they are baked through. Stick to recipes that have been devised specifically for gluten-free flour. If you are going to bake vegan, gluten-free cakes regularly, a pack of xanthan gum is a storecupboard essential. Just a tiny amount makes all the difference, helping pastries and doughs to hold together and stopping traybakes and sponges from being crumbly. But don't assume that using more than the recipe specifies will be a good thing – too much and your sponge cakes will be oddly rubbery.

CHAPTER 1

Cakes

PREP TIME: 1 hour

COOK TIME: 1–1¼ hours

SERVES: 8–12

Raspberry NEAPOLITAN CAKE

With three different layers and two kinds of filling, this cake takes time, but what better way to show somebody that you love them?

PINK LAYER

70 g/2½ oz raw beetroot

85 g/3 oz raspberries

vegan and gluten-free egg replacer, equivalent to 2 eggs

125 ml/4 fl oz gluten-free soya milk

1 tbsp vegan, gluten-free cider vinegar

125 g/4½ oz gluten-free self-raising flour

½ tsp xanthan gum

1 tsp gluten-free baking powder

½ tsp gluten-free cream of tartar

100 g/3½ oz vegan and gluten-free margarine, plus extra for greasing

225 g/8 oz caster sugar

1 tsp vanilla extract

VANILLA LAYER

200 g/7 oz gluten-free self-raising flour

½ tsp xanthan gum

115 g/4 oz caster sugar

1 tsp gluten-free baking powder

200 ml/7 fl oz gluten-free soya milk

75 ml/2½ fl oz rapeseed oil

2 tsp vanilla extract

CHOCOLATE LAYER

175 g/6 oz gluten-free self-raising flour

(ingredients continued on page 19)

1 Preheat the oven to 180°C/350°F/Gas Mark 4. Grease three 23-cm/9-inch sandwich tins and line with baking paper.

2 For the pink layer, trim, peel and grate the beetroot and put it into the bowl of a food processor with the raspberries. Process until smooth. Make up the egg replacer in a small bowl according to the packet instructions and beat it with a fork for a minute until bubbly.

3 Put the soya milk into a measuring jug, stir in the vinegar and set aside to curdle. Put the flour, xanthan gum, baking powder and cream of tartar into a large mixing bowl and stir together with a wooden spoon. In a separate bowl, cream the margarine and sugar together and beat in the egg replacer and vanilla extract.

4 Stir the soya milk mixture and the creamed margarine mixture into the dry ingredients and mix thoroughly. Pour in the beetroot purée and stir together with a wooden spoon until the mixture is thoroughly combined.

5 Spoon the mixture into one of the prepared tins and smooth the top. Bake in the preheated oven for 25–30 minutes, or until a skewer inserted into the cake comes out clean. Turn out onto a wire rack and leave to cool completely.

6 For the vanilla layer, put the flour, xanthan gum, sugar and baking powder into a large mixing bowl and stir together with a wooden spoon. Add the soya milk, oil and vanilla and stir together until just combined. Spoon into one of the prepared tins and bake for 20 minutes, or until golden and springy to the touch. Turn out onto a wire rack to cool.

7 For the chocolate layer, repeat step 6, including the cocoa powder with the dry ingredients.

30 g/1 oz vegan and gluten-free cocoa powder

½ tsp xanthan gum

115 g/4 oz caster sugar

1 tsp gluten-free baking powder

200 ml/7 fl oz gluten-free soya milk

75 ml/2½ fl oz rapeseed oil

1 tsp vanilla extract

VANILLA-RASPBERRY FILLING

25 g/1 oz vegan, gluten-free margarine

55 g/2 oz white vegetable shortening

375 g/13 oz vegan, gluten-free icing sugar

1 tsp vanilla extract

2–3 tbsp gluten-free soya milk

2 tbsp freeze-dried raspberry pieces

150 g/5½ oz fresh raspberries

CHOCOLATE FILLING

25 g/1 oz vegan, gluten-free margarine

55 g/2 oz white vegetable shortening

325 g/11½ oz vegan, gluten-free icing sugar

55 g/2 oz vegan and gluten-free cocoa powder

2–3 tbsp gluten-free soya milk

freeze-dried raspberry pieces and vegan and gluten-free icing sugar, to decorate

8 To make the raspberry filling, beat the margarine and vegetable shortening together with the icing sugar and vanilla. It's easiest to use a food mixer, but you can do it in a large mixing bowl with a fork. Add a little soya milk if necessary. When the mixture is smooth, stir in the freeze-dried raspberry pieces.

9 To make the chocolate filling, follow step 8 but add the cocoa powder at the same time as the icing sugar. When all three layers of the cake are cool, assemble the layers. Spread the pink cake with the raspberry filling. Add a layer of fresh raspberries. Sandwich with the chocolate cake and spread over the chocolate filling. Finish with the vanilla cake and decorate with icing sugar and freeze-dried raspberry pieces.

Cook's tip

Each layer of this cake should be baked separately so that the baking powder is still active when it goes into the oven. If your cake shows any signs of sagging in the middle, pile in some extra raspberries to hold it up!

2

4

5

PREP TIME: 25 minutes COOK TIME: 45–50 minutes SERVES: 8–10

Chocolate & Banana LOAF

Chunky almonds and dark chocolate pieces give this cake its home-baked character.

1 Preheat the oven to 180°C/350°F/Gas Mark 4. Grease a 900 g/2 lb loaf tin and line the base with baking paper.

2 Sift the flour, baking powder and bicarbonate of soda into a large mixing bowl. Stir in the sugar.

3 Stir the chocolate and the almonds into the dry ingredients.

4 Stir the bananas into the dry ingredients, along with the almond milk, oil and almond extract, and mix well with a wooden spoon.

5 Spoon the mixture into the prepared baking tin and smooth the top with a rubber spatula. Bake in the preheated oven for 45–50 minutes, or until a skewer inserted into the centre of the cake comes out clean. Leave the cake in the tin to firm up for 15 minutes, then transfer to a wire rack to cool.

vegan and gluten-free margarine, for greasing

250 g/9 oz gluten-free self-raising flour

1 tsp gluten-free baking powder

1 tsp gluten-free bicarbonate of soda

150 g/5½ oz brown sugar

85 g/3 oz vegan and gluten-free dark chocolate, roughly chopped

85 g/3 oz blanched almonds, roughly chopped

3 ripe unwaxed bananas, mashed

225 ml/8 fl oz almond milk

100 ml/3½ fl oz rapeseed oil

1 tsp almond extract

Cook's tip

Many gluten-free cakes of this size will benefit from the ingredient xanthan gum to prevent a powdery texture, but the mashed banana does the work in this recipe.

PREP TIME: 20 minutes   COOK TIME: 30–35 minutes   SERVES: 8–12

Maple & Pistachio BUNDT CAKE

This simple cake is wonderful with vegan and gluten-free vanilla ice cream and a fresh fruit salad.

- 300 g/10½ oz gluten-free self-raising flour
- 175 g/6 oz granulated sugar
- 1½ tsp gluten-free baking powder
- 85 g/3 oz shelled pistachios
- 300 ml/10 fl oz gluten-free soya milk
- 125 ml/4 fl oz rapeseed oil, plus extra for greasing
- 3 tbsp maple syrup, plus extra for drizzling
- 1 tbsp vanilla extract

1 Preheat the oven to 180°C/350°F/Gas Mark 4. Grease a 24-cm/9½-inch bundt tin.

2 Put the flour, sugar and baking powder in a large mixing bowl and stir together. Finely chop one third of the pistachios and set aside for decoration. Roughly chop the remaining pistachios and stir them into the dry ingredients.

3 Put the soya milk into a measuring jug and add the oil, maple syrup and vanilla extract.

4 Pour the wet ingredients into the bowl of dry ingredients and quickly mix with a wooden spoon until just combined. Spoon the mixture into the prepared tin and smooth the surface with a spatula. Bake in the preheated oven for 30–35 minutes, or until firm and golden. Leave the cake to cool in the tin for 10 minutes, then turn it out onto a wire rack to cool.

5 To decorate, transfer the cake to a serving plate, drizzle with maple syrup and scatter the reserved pistachios over the top.

2

3

4

Cook's tip

Use the best quality maple syrup you can – the taste makes all the difference when it's drizzled over this simple cake.

Cook's tip
Try substituting vegan rum for the amaretto to make a rum and sultana cake.

PREP TIME: 15 minutes, plus soaking

COOK TIME: 20–25 minutes

SERVES: 9

Almond & Amaretto CAKE

This moist and tasty almond cake is lovely served with a scoop of vegan and gluten-free ice cream and a drizzle of maple syrup.

- 30 g/1 oz sultanas
- 1 tbsp vegan amaretto
- vegan and gluten-free egg replacer, equivalent to 4 eggs
- 115 g/4 oz vegan and gluten-free margarine, plus extra for greasing
- 125 g/4½ oz caster sugar
- 40 g/1½ oz gluten-free self-raising flour
- 90 g/3¼ oz ground almonds
- 1 tsp gluten-free baking powder
- ½ tsp xanthan gum
- 1 tbsp toasted flaked almonds
- vegan and gluten-free ice cream and maple syrup, to serve (optional)

1 Preheat the oven to 180°C/350°F/Gas Mark 4. Grease a 20-cm/8-inch square cake tin and line with baking paper.

2 Put the sultanas into a small bowl with the amaretto and leave to soak for 30 minutes. Make up the egg replacer in a small bowl according to the packet instructions and beat it with a fork for a minute until bubbly.

3 Put the vegan margarine and sugar into a large mixing bowl and beat together with a wooden spoon until creamy. Mix in the egg replacer, then fold in the flour, ground almonds, baking powder and xanthan gum. Fold in the sultanas, along with any remaining liquid. Spoon the mixture into the prepared tin and smooth the top with a spatula.

4 Bake in the preheated oven for 20–25 minutes, or until golden and springy to the touch. Sprinkle with the toasted flaked almonds and leave to cool in the tin for 10 minutes. Transfer to a wire rack to cool completely before slicing and serving with ice cream and a drizzle of maple syrup, if desired.

PREP TIME: 20 minutes COOK TIME: 1¼–1½ hours SERVES: 10

Apricot & Apple SPICED LOAF

A slice of this fruity loaf is perfect when spread with your favourite non-dairy butter or vegan cream cheese.

- 100 g/3½ oz dried unwaxed apricots, diced
- 25 g/1 oz dried unwaxed apples, diced
- 25 g/1 oz sultanas
- 1 tsp ground cinnamon
- 1 tsp ground mixed spice
- vegan and gluten-free egg replacer, equivalent to 2 eggs
- 115 g/4 oz vegan and gluten-free margarine, plus extra for greasing
- 115 g/4 oz brown sugar
- 115 g/4 oz gluten-free self-raising flour
- 50 g/1¾ oz rice flour
- 1½ tsp gluten-free baking powder
- ½ tsp xanthan gum
- 4 tbsp gluten-free soya milk

1 Preheat the oven to 160°C/325°F/Gas Mark 3. Grease a 900-g/2-lb loaf tin and line with baking paper.

2 Place the dried apricot and apple into a small mixing bowl with the sultanas. Add the cinnamon and mixed spice and stir together. Make up the egg replacer in a small bowl according to the packet instructions and beat it with a fork for a minute until bubbly.

3 Put the vegan margarine and sugar into a large mixing bowl and beat together with a wooden spoon until creamy. Beat in the egg replacer. Gradually stir in the flours, baking powder and xanthan gum. Add enough of the soya milk to moisten the mixture – it should drop off a spoon easily.

4 Fold in the spiced dried fruits and spoon the mixture into the prepared loaf tin. Smooth the top with a spatula.

5 Bake in the preheated oven for 1¼–1½ hours, or until golden brown and firm to the touch. Leave the loaf to cool in the tin for 10 minutes before turning it out onto a wire rack to cool completely.

PREP TIME: 25 minutes   COOK TIME: 20 minutes   SERVES: 8–12

Fresh Fruit LAYER CAKE

This is a show-stopping layer cake that is perfect for a summer celebration. The maple-cashew filling is subtle so the fresh fruit flavours shine through.

400 g/14 oz gluten-free self-raising flour

225 g/8 oz granulated sugar

2 tsp gluten-free baking powder

400 ml/14 fl oz gluten-free soya milk

150 ml/5 fl oz rapeseed oil, plus extra for greasing

2 tbsp vanilla extract

450 g/1 lb fresh seasonal unwaxed fruit, chopped

vegan and gluten-free icing sugar, to decorate

MAPLE-CASHEW FILLING

200 g/7 oz cashews

350 g/12 oz extra firm silken tofu

3 tbsp maple syrup

1 tbsp rapeseed oil

1 tsp vanilla extract

1 Preheat the oven to 180°C/350°F/Gas Mark 4. Grease two 20-cm/8-inch sandwich tins and line with baking paper.

2 Put the flour, sugar and baking powder into a large mixing bowl and stir together with a wooden spoon. Add the soya milk, oil and vanilla, stir quickly to combine the wet and dry ingredients and then spoon the mixture into the prepared tins and smooth the tops with a rubber spatula. Bake in the preheated oven for 20 minutes, or until a skewer inserted into the cakes comes out clean. Turn the cakes out onto a wire rack and leave to cool completely.

3 To make the filling, put the cashews into a food processor and process them to a fine powder. Add the tofu, maple syrup, oil and vanilla, and process to a thick cream.

4 Carefully slice each cake in half to make four layers. Put one piece of cake onto a serving plate and build up the cake with layers of cashew cream and fresh fruit. Sift a little icing sugar over the top of the cake and then pile some fresh fruit on top before serving.

Cook's tip
It is best to layer up this cake on the plate or serving display that you'll be presenting it on, as it's quite tall and tricky to move once it's all assembled!

PREP TIME: 20 minutes COOK TIME: 45 minutes SERVES: 12

Raspberry Chocolate CAKE

This is a deliciously decadent-looking cake, with a rich chocolate icing on top and fresh, zingy raspberries.

- vegan and gluten-free margarine, for greasing
- 300 g/10½ oz gluten-free plain flour
- 50 g/1¾ oz vegan and gluten-free cocoa powder
- ½ tsp xanthan gum
- 1 tsp gluten-free baking powder
- 1 tsp gluten-free bicarbonate of soda
- ½ tsp salt
- 300 g/10½ oz granulated sugar
- 375 ml/13 fl oz gluten-free soya milk
- 125 ml/4 fl oz rapeseed oil
- 7 tbsp gluten-free seedless raspberry jam
- 1 tsp vanilla extract

ICING

- 45 ml/1½ fl oz gluten-free soya milk
- 85 g/3 oz vegan and gluten-free dark chocolate, broken into small pieces
- 60 g/2¼ oz vegan and gluten-free icing sugar
- 1 tbsp maple syrup
- fresh raspberries, to decorate

1 Preheat the oven to 180°C/350°F/Gas Mark 4. Grease a 23-cm/9-inch round cake tin and line with baking paper.

2 Sift the flour, cocoa, xanthan gum, baking powder and bicarbonate of soda into a large mixing bowl and stir in the salt and sugar. Pour the soya milk into a medium saucepan and add the oil, raspberry jam and vanilla extract. Place over a medium heat and whisk to combine. Stir into the dry ingredients and mix thoroughly.

3 Transfer to the prepared cake tin and bake in the preheated oven for 45 minutes, or until a skewer inserted into the centre comes out clean. Turn out and leave to cool completely on a wire rack before icing.

4 To make the icing, heat the soya milk in a small saucepan over a medium heat until it reaches boiling point, then drop the chocolate into the pan and stir until completely melted. Remove from the heat and whisk in the icing sugar and maple syrup. Set aside to cool before icing the cake, using a palette knife. Top with a few fresh raspberries before slicing and serving.

Cook's tip

Substitute unwaxed, gluten-free orange marmalade for the raspberry jam and decorate with sliced unwaxed oranges dipped in melted vegan and gluten-free chocolate.

3

5

6

PREP TIME: 20 minutes COOK TIME: 35–40 minutes SERVES: 6–8

Blueberry POLENTA CAKE

Grated apple makes this cake sweet, moist and moreish!

- vegan and gluten-free margarine, for greasing
- 250 g/9 oz quick-cook polenta
- 3 tsp gluten-free baking powder
- 1 tsp xanthan gum
- vegan and gluten-free egg replacer, equivalent to 3 eggs
- 175 g/6 oz golden caster sugar
- 125 ml/4 fl oz rapeseed oil
- zest of 1 unwaxed lemon
- 1 unwaxed apple
- 125 g/4½ oz blueberries

1 Preheat the oven to 180°C/350°F/Gas Mark 4. Grease a 20-cm/8-inch round, loose-based cake tin and line with baking paper.

2 Put the polenta, baking powder and xanthan gum into a large mixing bowl and mix together thoroughly with a wooden spoon.

3 Make up the egg replacer in a small bowl according to the packet instructions and beat it with a fork for a minute until bubbly. Put the sugar and oil into a separate mixing bowl and beat them together with a fork. Gradually add the egg replacer and lemon zest and continue to beat until the ingredients are well combined.

4 Peel, core and grate the apple and mix into the wet ingredients with a wooden spoon.

5 Pour the wet ingredients onto the polenta mixture and stir well with a wooden spoon to combine.

6 Spoon the mixture into the prepared cake tin and smooth the top with the back of a spoon. Sprinkle the blueberries on top of the cake and gently press them onto the surface of the mixture.

7 Bake in the preheated oven for 35–40 minutes, or until golden and cooked through. Allow the cake to cool completely before removing from the tin.

Cook's tip

Choose a light rapeseed oil that will not affect the flavour of the cake.

PREP TIME: 20 minutes COOK TIME: 1 hour SERVES: 8–12

Carrot & Walnut CAKE

It's easy to make a delicious carrot cake with vegan cream cheese – just try not to eat it all before the cake is cool enough to frost!

vegan and gluten-free margarine, for greasing

225 g/8 oz gluten-free self-raising flour

2 tsp gluten-free baking powder

115 g/4 oz brown sugar

2 tsp ground cinnamon

1 tsp ground nutmeg

85 g/3 oz walnuts, roughly chopped

225 g/8 oz carrots, grated

125 ml/4 fl oz maple syrup

125 ml/4 fl oz rapeseed oil

CREAM CHEESE FROSTING

115 g/4 oz vegan and gluten-free cream cheese

55 g/2 oz vegan and gluten-free margarine

225 g/8 oz vegan and gluten-free icing sugar

1 Preheat the oven to 160°C/325°F/Gas Mark 3. Grease an 18-cm/7-inch round, loose-based cake tin and line with baking paper.

2 Sift the flour and baking powder into a large mixing bowl. Stir in the sugar, cinnamon, nutmeg and walnuts and mix well with a wooden spoon.

3 Stir the carrots into the dry ingredients, along with the maple syrup and rapeseed oil, and mix well with a wooden spoon.

4 Spoon the mixture into the prepared cake tin, smooth the top with a rubber spatula and bake in the preheated oven for 1 hour, or until a skewer inserted into the centre of the cake comes out clean. Leave the cake in the tin to firm up for 10 minutes, then transfer to a wire rack and allow to cool completely before frosting.

5 To make the frosting, beat the cream cheese, margarine and icing sugar together until smooth. Using an electric food mixer or a hand-held electric mixer is easiest for this, but you can do it with a fork if necessary. Spread the filling generously on the top of the cake, and on the sides too if you like, and swirl the surface into an attractive pattern with a fork. Leave to set before serving.

2

3

5

Cook's tip

To make a sandwich cake, carefully slice the cake in half and sandwich with the cream cheese frosting. Using two sandwich tins tends to make the cake rather dry and hard around the edges.

Cook's tip

This cake would also be lovely served as a dessert, with vegan and gluten-free custard.

PREP TIME: 20 minutes COOK TIME: 1 hour SERVES: 12

Mixed Berry BUNDT CAKE

This cake is bursting with fresh summer flavours, with raspberries, blueberries and blackberries, as well as coconut.

- 350 g/12 oz gluten-free plain flour, plus extra for dusting
- ½ tsp xanthan gum
- 2 tsp gluten-free baking powder
- 1 tsp gluten-free bicarbonate of soda
- 400 g/14 oz caster sugar
- 55 g/2 oz desiccated coconut
- 500 ml/18 fl oz gluten-free soya milk
- 150 ml/5 fl oz rapeseed oil, plus extra for greasing
- 2 tsp vanilla extract
- 1 tsp salt
- 250 g/9 oz mixed berries, such as raspberries, blueberries and blackberries, plus extra to serve
- vegan and gluten-free icing sugar, to dust
- vegan and gluten-free vanilla ice cream, to serve (optional)

1 Preheat the oven to 180°C/350°F/Gas Mark 4. Grease and flour a 24-cm/9½-inch bundt tin.

2 Sift together the flour, xanthan gum, baking powder and bicarbonate of soda into a large bowl and stir in the sugar and coconut. Add the soya milk, oil and vanilla extract. Whisk together until smooth – the mixture will look like a thick batter. Stir in the salt and berries.

3 Pour the batter into the prepared bundt tin. Bake in the preheated oven for 1 hour, or until a skewer inserted into the cake comes out clean. Leave to cool in the tin for 5 minutes before turning out onto a wire rack.

4 When the cake has cooled, dust it with icing sugar and fill the centre with more fresh berries. Slice and serve with a scoop of ice cream, if desired.

PREP TIME: 20 minutes   COOK TIME: 25–30 minutes   SERVES: 8

Fig Upside-Down CAKE

What better way to enjoy the beautiful colour of fresh figs than by using them in an upside-down cake?

- vegan and gluten-free margarine, for greasing
- 3 tbsp brown sugar
- 4 fresh, unwaxed figs, halved vertically
- zest of 1 unwaxed orange
- 200 g/7 oz gluten-free self-raising flour
- 125 g/4½ oz granulated sugar
- 1 tsp gluten-free baking powder
- 1 tsp ground cinnamon
- 200 ml/7 fl oz gluten-free soya milk
- 90 ml/3 fl oz rapeseed oil

1 Preheat the oven to 180°C/350°F/Gas Mark 4. Grease a 20-cm/8-inch round cake tin and line with baking paper.

2 Sprinkle the brown sugar into the base of the prepared tin. Arrange the figs on top of the sugar in the tin, cut-side down. Sprinkle the orange zest over the figs.

3 Put the flour into a large mixing bowl and stir in the granulated sugar, baking powder and cinnamon.

4 Mix the soya milk and oil together in a measuring jug. Pour the wet ingredients over the dry ingredients and mix together quickly, with a rubber spatula, until just combined. Spoon the cake mix into the tin, carefully covering the figs, and smooth the top.

5 Bake in the preheated oven for 25–30 minutes, or until a skewer inserted into the centre of the cake comes out clean. Allow the cake to cool in the tin for 5 minutes then turn it out onto a serving plate. This cake is best served warm.

Cook's tip

Turn the cake out onto a serving plate, not a wire rack, so that you catch any juices from the fig topping. These juices can then be drizzled back over the cake.

2

3

4

Cook's tip

You can also choose pears with rosy skins for a prettier, pink effect on the cake.

PREP TIME: 30 minutes COOK TIME: 1¼ hours SERVES: 12

Pear & Pecan CAKE

A topping of oven-roasted pears makes this a moist cake with a nutty texture.

vegan and gluten-free margarine, for greasing
100 g/3½ oz pecan nuts
200 g/7 oz gluten-free self-raising flour
115 g/4 oz granulated sugar
1 tsp gluten-free baking powder
200 ml/7 fl oz gluten-free soya milk
75 ml/2½ fl oz rapeseed oil
2 tbsp maple syrup
1 tsp vanilla extract

TOPPING

2 unwaxed pears, halved, cored and sliced
25 g/1 oz caster sugar
juice of ½ an unwaxed lemon
25 g/1 oz vegan and gluten-free margarine
25 g/1 oz pecan nut halves

1 Preheat the oven to 180°C/350°F/Gas Mark 4. Grease a 23-cm/9-inch round, loose-based cake tin.

2 Divide the pecans into two equal portions. Chop one portion very finely. Put the finely chopped pecans into the prepared cake tin and tip the tin so that the chopped nuts stick to the greased base and sides of the tin. Tip any spare nuts out onto a plate.

3 Put the flour, sugar and baking powder into a large mixing bowl and stir together. Chop the remaining pecans roughly and stir them into the dry ingredients along with any of the leftover finely chopped pecans.

4 Put the soya milk into a measuring jug and add the oil, maple syrup and vanilla extract.

5 Pour the wet ingredients into the bowl of dry ingredients and quickly mix with a wooden spoon until just combined. Spoon the mixture into the prepared tin and smooth the surface with a spatula. Bake in the preheated oven for 35–40 minutes, or until firm and golden. Leave the cake to cool in the tin for 10 minutes, then turn it out onto a wire rack to cool. Leave the oven on.

6 To make the topping, place the pears in the bottom of a large baking dish. Sprinkle with the sugar and lemon juice and dot with margarine. Bake for 30 minutes, basting every 10 minutes, then set aside to cool.

7 Decorate the cake by overlapping the pear slices in a circle around the edge and then fill the gap in the centre with pecan halves.

PREP TIME: 30 minutes COOK TIME: 25–30 minutes SERVES: 8–12

Strawberry RED VELVET CAKE

This spectacular cake owes its rich, red colour to beetroot, but tastes of raspberries and strawberries.

140 g/5 oz raw beetroot

175 g/6 oz raspberries

vegan and gluten-free egg replacer, equivalent to 4 eggs

225 ml/8 fl oz gluten-free soya milk

2 tbsp vegan and gluten-free cider vinegar

280 g/10 oz gluten-free self-raising flour

3 tbsp vegan and gluten-free cocoa powder

1 tsp xanthan gum

2 tsp gluten-free baking powder

1 tsp gluten-free cream of tartar

175 g/6 oz vegan and gluten-free margarine, plus extra for greasing

450 g/1 lb caster sugar

1 tsp vanilla extract

FILLING

25 g/1 oz vegan and gluten-free margarine

25 g/1 oz white vegetable shortening

55 g/2 oz vegan and gluten-free cream cheese

375 g/13 oz vegan and gluten-free icing sugar, plus extra for dusting

1 tsp vanilla extract

2–3 tbsp gluten-free soya milk

2 tbsp freeze-dried strawberry pieces

150 g/5½ oz fresh strawberries

1 Trim, peel and grate the beetroot and put it into the bowl of a food processor with the raspberries. Process until smooth.

2 Preheat the oven to 180°C/350°F/Gas Mark 4. Grease two 20-cm/8-inch sandwich tins and line with baking paper. Make up the egg replacer in a small bowl according to the packet instructions and beat it with a fork for a minute until bubbly.

3 Put the soya milk into a measuring jug, stir in the vinegar and set aside to curdle. Put the flour, cocoa powder, xanthan gum, baking powder and cream of tartar into a large mixing bowl and stir together with a wooden spoon. In a separate bowl, cream the margarine and sugar together and beat in the egg replacer and vanilla extract.

4 Stir the milk mixture and the margarine mixture into the dry ingredients and mix thoroughly. Pour in the beetroot and raspberry purée and stir together with a wooden spoon until the mixture is thoroughly combined.

5 Spoon the mixture into the prepared tins and smooth the tops with a spatula. Bake in the preheated oven for 25–30 minutes, or until a skewer inserted into the cakes comes out clean. Turn out onto a wire rack and leave to cool completely.

6 To make the filling, beat the margarine, vegetable shortening and cream cheese together with the icing sugar and vanilla. It's easiest to use a food mixer, but you can do it in a large mixing bowl with a fork. Add a little soya milk if necessary. When the mixture is smooth, stir in the freeze-dried strawberry pieces.

7 Spread the bottom layer of the cake with the filling. Cut the fresh strawberries in half and arrange them over the layer of icing, pressing them in. Sandwich with the second layer of the cake and dust with icing sugar to serve.

Cook's tip
The raspberries cover any beetroot taste in this cake. They also create an acidic mixture which helps prevent the beetroot from browning as it bakes.

PREP TIME: 20 minutes, plus soaking

COOK TIME: 30 minutes

SERVES: 12

Vegan Ricotta CAKE

A contradiction in terms? A vegan 'ricotta' made with cashews and dates works perfectly in this cake.

VEGAN RICOTTA

85 g/3 oz raw cashew nuts

30 g/1 oz stoned unwaxed dates, roughly chopped

vegan and gluten-free egg replacer, equivalent to 2 eggs

125 g/4½ oz vegan and gluten-free margarine, plus extra for greasing

185 g/6½ oz golden caster sugar

200 g/7 oz gluten-free plain flour

2 tsp gluten-free baking powder

1 tsp xanthan gum

2 tsp instant coffee powder

1 To make the ricotta, soak the cashews in 125 ml/4 fl oz water for 30 minutes. Put the dates into the bowl of a food processor along with the cashews and the soaking water. Process to a thick, smooth consistency.

2 Preheat the oven to 180°C/350°F/Gas Mark 4. Grease a 23-cm/9-inch square baking tin and line with baking paper. Make up the egg replacer in a small bowl according to the packet instructions and beat it with a fork for a minute until bubbly.

3 In a large mixing bowl, cream the margarine and sugar together with a wooden spoon. Beat in the vegan ricotta and egg replacer. Add in the flour, baking powder, xanthan gum and coffee powder and mix thoroughly.

4 Spoon the mixture into the prepared tin and smooth the top with a spatula. Bake in the preheated oven for 30 minutes, or until golden and springy to the touch. Leave to cool in the tin for 5 minutes before transferring to a wire rack to cool completely.

1

3

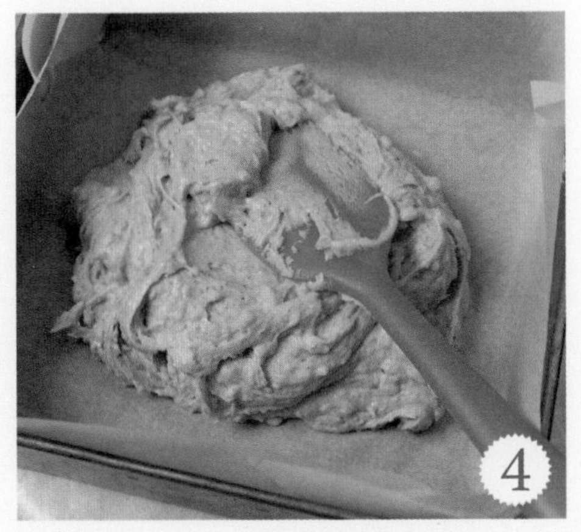
4

PREP TIME: 30 minutes COOK TIME: 25–30 minutes SERVES: 8–12

Chocolate Mint MARBLE CAKE

This is a fun-looking cake with swirls of chocolate and crunchy green sugar sprinkles that would be good for serving at a teenager's party.

225 g/8 oz gluten-free self-raising flour
115 g/4 oz granulated sugar
1½ tsp gluten-free baking powder
200 ml/7 fl oz gluten-free soya milk
75 ml/2½ fl oz rapeseed oil, plus extra for greasing
25 g/1 oz vegan and gluten-free cocoa powder
½ tsp peppermint essence
½ tsp green food colouring

TOPPING

55 g/2 oz vegan and gluten-free dark chocolate, broken into pieces
1 tbsp gluten-free soya cream
2 tbsp granulated sugar
½ tsp peppermint essence
¼ tsp green food colouring

1 Preheat the oven to 180°C/350°F/Gas Mark 4. Grease a 23-cm/9-inch round, loose-based cake tin.

2 Put the flour, sugar and baking powder in a large mixing bowl and stir together with a wooden spoon.

3 Put the soya milk into a measuring jug and add the oil.

4 Pour the wet ingredients into the bowl of dry ingredients and quickly mix with a wooden spoon until just combined. Spoon half of the mixture into another mixing bowl.

5 Add the cocoa to one bowl and the peppermint essence and green food colouring to the other. Mix quickly to combine, then spoon the mixtures into the prepared tin. Use a knife to swirl through the mixtures, and smooth the surface with a spatula. Bake in the preheated oven for 25–30 minutes, or until firm and golden. Leave the cake to cool in the tin for 10 minutes, then turn it out onto a wire rack to cool before decorating.

6 To make the topping, melt the dark chocolate with the soya cream in a microwave or in a heatproof bowl set over a saucepan of gently simmering water. Put the granulated sugar into a bowl and mix in the peppermint essence and green food colouring. Drizzle the melted chocolate over the cake and sprinkle the peppermint sugar over the top. Leave the chocolate to cool and set before serving.

Cook's tip

You can make your own vegan after-dinner mints by stirring this peppermint sugar into melted chocolate and spooning it onto a silicon baking sheet to set.

4

5

6

Cook's tip
Black or red cherries work well visually with this cake. Be sure to use the best quality cherry jam you can find – home made would be perfect!

PREP TIME: 20 minutes COOK TIME: 30–35 minutes SERVES: 8–12

Cherry & Vanilla BUNDT CAKE

Filled with luscious ripe cherries, this cake makes a beautiful centrepiece for a summer afternoon tea.

- 300 g/10½ oz gluten-free self-raising flour
- 175 g/6 oz granulated sugar
- 1½ tsp gluten-free baking powder
- 300 ml/10 fl oz gluten-free soya milk
- 125 ml/4 fl oz rapeseed oil, plus extra for greasing
- 1 tbsp vanilla extract
- 325 g/11½ oz gluten-free, unwaxed cherry jam
- 250 g/9 oz fresh, unwaxed cherries

1 Preheat the oven to 180°C/350°F/Gas Mark 4. Grease a 24-cm/9½-inch bundt tin.

2 Put the flour, sugar and baking powder in a large mixing bowl and stir together with a wooden spoon.

3 Put the soya milk into a measuring jug and add the oil and vanilla extract. Stir in 3 tablespoons of cherry jam. Set aside 5 tablespoons of cherry jam to use to decorate the cake once it is baked.

4 Pour the wet ingredients into the bowl of dry ingredients and quickly mix with a wooden spoon until just combined. Spoon half of the mixture into the prepared tin. Dot the surface of the cake mixture with teaspoonfuls of the remaining cherry jam. Cover with the rest of the cake mix. Bake for 30–35 minutes, or until firm and golden. Allow the cake to cool in the tin for 10 minutes, then turn out onto a wire rack to cool.

5 Put the reserved jam into a small saucepan with 1 tablespoon of water and heat gently to melt the jam into a runny syrup. Strain the syrup through a sieve, discard the solids and set the syrup aside to cool.

6 When the cake is cool, transfer it to a serving plate and fill the hole in the centre with fresh cherries. Drizzle the cake and the fresh cherries with the cherry jam syrup just before serving.

PREP TIME: 25 minutes COOK TIME: 30 minutes SERVES: 8–12

Chocolate Fudge CAKE

The texture of this cake is like a brownie – soft inside, with a slightly crispy edge and a cracked surface that hints at the fudgy chocolate delights within.

- 125 g/4½ oz vegan and gluten-free dark chocolate, broken into pieces
- 125 g/4½ oz vegan and gluten-free margarine, plus extra for greasing
- 300 g/10½ oz caster sugar
- 1 tsp vegan glycerine
- ½ tsp vanilla extract
- vegan and gluten-free egg replacer, equivalent to 2 eggs
- 100 ml/3½ fl oz gluten-free soya cream
- 100 g/3½ oz rice flour
- 100 g/3½ oz gluten-free self-raising flour
- ½ tsp xanthan gum
- ½ tsp gluten-free baking powder
- ½ tsp gluten-free bicarbonate of soda

FROSTING

- 150 g/5½ oz vegan and gluten-free dark chocolate, broken into pieces
- 150 ml/5 fl oz gluten-free soya cream
- 200 g/7 oz vegan and gluten-free icing sugar, plus extra to decorate
- 100 g/3½ oz vegan and gluten-free margarine

1 Preheat the oven to 180°C/350°F/Gas Mark 4. Grease two 20-cm/8-inch sandwich tins and line with baking paper.

2 Place the chocolate in a small heatproof bowl over a saucepan of gently simmering water. Melt the chocolate and then set aside to cool.

3 In a large mixing bowl, cream the margarine, sugar, glycerine and vanilla together. Make up the egg replacer in a small bowl according to the packet instructions and beat it with a fork for a minute until bubbly. Add the egg replacer to the mixing bowl and beat until it is light and fluffy. Stir in the soya cream and the cooled chocolate. Fold in the rice flour, self-raising flour, xanthan gum, baking powder and bicarbonate of soda.

4 Spoon the mixture into the prepared tins and smooth the tops with a rubber spatula. Bake in the preheated oven for 30 minutes, or until a skewer inserted into the cakes comes out clean. Leave to cool in the tins for 30 minutes, then turn them out onto a wire rack. Leave to cool completely.

5 To make the frosting, place the chocolate and soya cream in a small heatproof bowl over a saucepan of gently simmering water. Stir until the chocolate is melted and then set aside to cool.

6 Cream the icing sugar and margarine together in a small bowl then pour in the cooled chocolate mixture. Beat well for 2–3 minutes, or until it thickens to a fudgy consistency.

7 Sandwich the cakes together with the frosting and sift a little icing sugar over the top of the cake before serving.

Cook's tip
For any serious chocaholics, you could always double the quantities of frosting and cover the top and sides of the cake too for a truly decadent treat!

4

5

7

PREP TIME: 1 hour COOK TIME: 40 minutes SERVES: 8–12

Orange Olive Oil CAKE

This moist cake is rich with Mediterranean flavours to bring some sunshine to your table whatever the time of year!

55 g/2 oz pine nuts
175 g/6 oz gluten-free plain flour
1 tsp xanthan gum
2 tsp gluten-free baking powder
55 g/2 oz ground almonds
225 g/8 oz caster sugar
zest and juice of 1 unwaxed orange
vegan and gluten-free egg replacer, equivalent to 4 eggs
90 ml/3 fl oz almond milk
150 ml/5 fl oz extra virgin olive oil, plus extra for greasing
75 ml/2½ fl oz coconut oil

CRYSTALLIZED ORANGE SLICES

1 large unwaxed orange, scrubbed
100 g/3½ oz granulated sugar
350 ml/12 fl oz water

1 Preheat the oven to 180°C/350°F/Gas Mark 4. Grease a 23-cm/9-inch round, springform cake tin and line with baking paper.

2 Put the pine nuts into a heavy-based saucepan and warm them gently over a low heat, stirring constantly with a wooden spatula until they begin to turn golden. Tip them onto a plate and set aside.

3 Sift the flour, xanthan gum and baking powder into a large mixing bowl. Stir in the ground almonds, caster sugar and orange zest.

4 Make up the egg replacer in a small bowl according to the packet instructions and beat it with a fork for a minute until bubbly.

5 Add the almond milk, olive oil and coconut oil to the dry ingredients and mix well. Fold in the egg replacer with a rubber spatula. Finally, stir in the orange juice and toasted pine nuts.

6 Spoon the mixture into the prepared cake tin and smooth the top with a rubber spatula. Bake in the preheated oven for 40 minutes, or until a skewer inserted into the cake comes out clean. Release the sides of the cake tin and transfer the cake to a wire rack to cool.

7 To make the orange slices, cut the orange into circles around 5 mm/ ¼ inch thick and halve each circle. Put the sugar into a heavy-based saucepan with the water and bring to the boil, stirring frequently to ensure that the sugar is dissolved. Add the orange slices and simmer on a medium heat for about 20 minutes, turning the oranges occasionally, until the sugar water has reduced to a thin syrup. Reduce the heat and continue to cook for a further 10 minutes, until the syrup is thick. Transfer the oranges to a wire rack to cool.

8 Prick the cake with a skewer and slowly pour over the warm orange syrup. When the orange slices are cool, arrange them in a decorative pattern on top of the cake.

Cook's tip

For a quicker alternative to the orange slices, pour 2 tbsp vegan orange liqueur over the cake, allow it to cool and dust with vegan and gluten-free icing sugar.

CHAPTER 2

Small Cakes

PREP TIME: 20 minutes COOK TIME: 18–20 minutes MAKES: 12

Cookies & Cream CUPCAKES

Perhaps it's the unexpected crunch inside these cupcakes that makes them such a firm family favourite!

250 ml/9 fl oz gluten-free soya milk

1 tsp vegan and gluten-free cider vinegar

150 g/5½ oz caster sugar

75 ml/2½ fl oz rapeseed oil

1 tsp vanilla extract

150 g/5½ oz gluten-free plain flour

25 g/1 oz vegan and gluten-free cocoa powder

¾ tsp gluten-free bicarbonate of soda

½ tsp gluten-free baking powder

70 g/2½ oz vegan and gluten-free cookies, chopped (see tip on right)

TOPPING

35 g/1¼ oz vegan and gluten-free margarine

35 g/1¼ oz white vegetable shortening

300 g/10½ oz vegan and gluten-free icing sugar

¾ tsp vanilla extract

75 ml/2½ fl oz gluten-free soya cream

35 g/1¼ oz vegan and gluten-free cookies, chopped

1 Preheat the oven to 180°C/350°F/Gas Mark 4. Line a 12-hole cupcake tin with paper cases.

2 Put the soya milk into a measuring jug, stir in the vinegar and set aside for a few minutes to curdle.

3 Put the sugar, oil and vanilla into a large mixing bowl and beat together. Pour in the milk and vinegar, mix thoroughly and then add the flour, cocoa powder, bicarbonate of soda and baking powder. Stir until the ingredients are just combined, then fold in the cookie crumbs.

4 Divide the mixture evenly between the paper cases and bake in the preheated oven for 18–20 minutes, or until springy to the touch and golden. Transfer to a wire rack to cool completely before icing.

5 To make the topping, beat the margarine and vegetable shortening together, then mix in the icing sugar and the vanilla. Gradually add the soya cream to achieve a thick pipeable consistency. Pipe or spoon the icing generously over the cupcakes and sprinkle with cookie crumbs.

Cook's tip

If you are unsure of which cookies to use, the chocolate cookies used to make the Ice-cream Sandwiches on page 100 would work very well in this recipe.

PREP TIME: 25 minutes　　COOK TIME: 18–20 minutes　　MAKES: 12

Pink Champagne CUPCAKES

Celebration cupcakes that aren't too sweet – and they taste just delicious with a glass of pink champagne!

90 ml/3 fl oz gluten-free soya milk

1 tsp vegan and gluten-free cider vinegar

25 g/1 oz caster sugar

50 ml/2 fl oz rapeseed oil

½ tsp vanilla extract

90 ml/3 fl oz vegan sparkling rosé wine

125 g/4½ oz gluten-free plain flour

½ tsp gluten-free bicarbonate of soda

½ tsp gluten-free baking powder

½ tsp salt

1 tbsp freeze-dried strawberry pieces

TOPPING

50 g/1¾ oz vegan and gluten-free margarine

50 g/1¾ oz white vegetable shortening

650 g/1 lb 7 oz vegan and gluten-free icing sugar

50 ml/2 fl oz vegan sparkling rosé wine

1 tbsp gluten-free strawberry jam

freeze-dried strawberry pieces, to decorate

1 Preheat the oven to 180°C/350°F/Gas Mark 4. Line a 12-hole cupcake tin with paper cases.

2 Put the soya milk into a measuring jug, stir in the vinegar and set aside for a few minutes to curdle.

3 Put the sugar, oil and vanilla into a large mixing bowl and beat together. Pour in the milk and vinegar and the wine and mix thoroughly. Add the flour, bicarbonate of soda, baking powder and salt and mix thoroughly. Finally, fold in the strawberry pieces.

4 Divide the mixture evenly between the paper cases. Bake in the preheated oven for 18–20 minutes, or until springy to the touch and golden. Transfer to a wire rack to cool completely.

5 To make the topping, beat the margarine, vegetable shortening and 500 g/1 lb 2 oz of the icing sugar together. Add the wine and jam. Mix well and beat in sufficient additional icing sugar to reach a pipeable consistency. Pipe generous swirls of icing onto the cakes and decorate with a scattering of freeze-dried strawberry pieces.

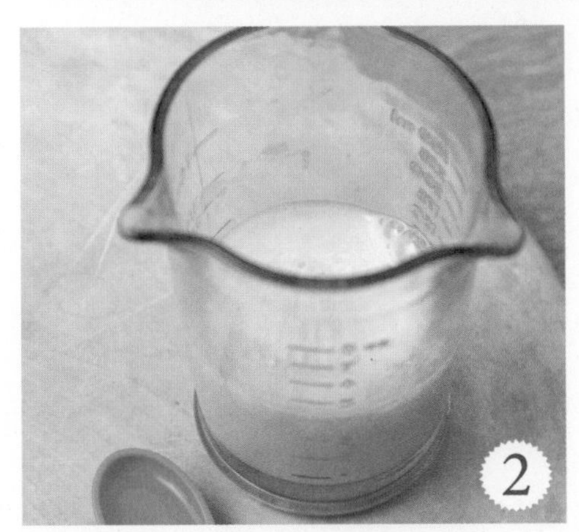
2

3

5

Cook's tip

If you don't have coffee essence, you could always mix a teaspoon of instant coffee granules with two teaspoons of cold water and use this mixture instead.

PREP TIME: 40 minutes   COOK TIME: 15–20 minutes   MAKES: 12

Coffee & Salted Caramel CUPCAKES

If you're baking to impress, these stunning cupcakes are the perfect showcase for your talents.

150 g/5½ oz gluten-free self-raising flour

85 g/3 oz caster sugar

½ tsp gluten-free baking powder

150 ml/5 fl oz gluten-free soya milk

4 tbsp rapeseed oil

2 tsp gluten-free coffee essence

SALTED SUGAR SHARDS (OPTIONAL)

25 g/1 oz roasted hazelnuts, chopped

¼ tsp sea salt

100 g/3½ oz caster sugar

SALTED CARAMEL

100 g/3½ oz caster sugar

100 g/3½ oz agave nectar

25 g/1 oz vegan and gluten-free margarine

5 tbsp coconut cream

½ tsp vanilla extract

¼ tsp sea salt

1 Preheat the oven to 180°C/350°F/Gas Mark 4. Line a 12-hole cupcake tin with paper cases.

2 Put the flour, caster sugar and baking powder into a large mixing bowl and stir together with a wooden spoon. Stir the soya milk, rapeseed oil and coffee essence into the dry ingredients. Divide the mixture between the paper cases and bake in the preheated oven for 15–20 minutes, or until a skewer inserted comes out clean. Transfer to a wire rack to cool. When the cakes are cool, use a melon baller or a teaspoon to scoop out a circular well in the top of each one. Discard the scooped out cake pieces.

3 To make the sugar shards, if using, cover a baking sheet with foil. Scatter the hazelnuts and salt over the foil. Put the caster sugar into a small saucepan with 100 ml/3½ fl oz cold water and heat gently, stirring frequently, until the sugar is completely dissolved. Increase the heat and bring the mixture to the boil, then keep it on a gentle boil, stirring continuously, for 5 minutes, or until it is syrupy. Carefully pour the syrup over the nuts and salt to make a thin layer and set aside to cool. When completely cool, carefully peel the foil off the sugar and use a sharp knife to break the sugar into shards.

4 To make the caramel, put the sugar, agave nectar, margarine and coconut cream into a saucepan and heat gently to melt the ingredients together. Keep stirring the mixture until the sugar dissolves, then increase the temperature and gradually bring the mixture to 113°C/235°F – 'soft ball' stage. If you don't have a sugar thermometer, you can test the caramel by chilling a plate in the refrigerator for a few minutes then putting a blob of caramel onto it. If it immediately forms a skin and holds its shape, it's ready. Take it off the heat and stir in the vanilla extract and salt.

5 Spoon the warm caramel into the wells in the cupcakes, taking care not to over-fill them. Place a sugar shard into the caramel on each cake while it is still warm. Set the cakes aside to cool. Serve the cupcakes within the hour, as the sugar shards will begin to dissolve if the cakes are left for longer.

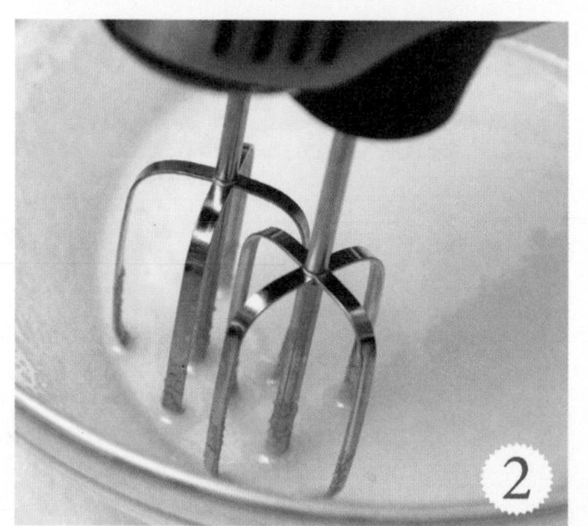
2

4

6

PREP TIME: 15–20 minutes COOK TIME: 25 minutes MAKES: 12

Green Tea CUPCAKES

A subtle green tea flavour makes these eye-catching cakes perfect to serve at the end of an Eastern-style banquet.

1 Preheat the oven to 180°C/350°F/Gas Mark 4. Line a 12-hole muffin tin with paper cases.

2 Make up the egg replacer in a small bowl according to the packet instructions and beat it with a fork for a minute until bubbly. Put the sugar and egg replacer into the bowl of a food mixer fitted with a whisk and beat on high speed for a minute. Alternatively, put the sugar and egg replacer into a large mixing bowl and beat with a hand whisk until frothy.

3 Sieve the flour, baking powder and xanthan gum into a large mixing bowl. Add the sugar mixture and stir in the matcha green tea powder.

4 Put the oil and rice milk into a large jug and stir with a metal spoon. Pour over the flour mixture and mix thoroughly.

5 Divide the mixture equally between the paper cases and bake in the preheated oven for 25 minutes, or until a skewer inserted into the centre of a cupcake comes out clean. Transfer to a wire rack to cool completely before frosting.

6 To make the frosting, put the margarine, vegetable shortening, matcha green tea powder and icing sugar in a large mixing bowl and cream together. A hand-held electric mixer is easiest for this, but it can also be done with a fork. Gradually beat in the rice milk until quite firm. Spoon the frosting into a piping bag. Decorate each cupcake with a generous swirl of frosting and a sprinkle of pistachios.

vegan and gluten-free egg replacer, equivalent to 2 eggs

175 g/6 oz caster sugar

175 g/6 oz gluten-free self-raising flour

1½ tsp gluten-free baking powder

½ tsp xanthan gum

4 tsp matcha green tea powder

125 ml/4 fl oz rapeseed oil

125 ml/4 fl oz rice milk

FROSTING

70 g/2½ oz vegan and gluten-free margarine

70 g/2½ oz white vegetable shortening

2 tsp matcha green tea powder

600 g/1 lb 5 oz vegan and gluten-free icing sugar

4 tbsp rice milk

25 g/1 oz shelled pistachio nuts, finely chopped

ME: 20–25 minutes COOK TIME: 20–25 minutes MAKES: 12

Raspberry & Dark Chocolate CUPCAKES

These pretty cupcakes have a combination of thick, rich chocolate and shocking pink sprinkles that makes them perfect for a girls' night in!

- vegan and gluten-free egg replacer, equivalent to 2 eggs
- 175 g/6 oz caster sugar
- 1 tsp vegan glycerine
- 150 g/5½ oz gluten-free self-raising flour
- 1 tsp gluten-free baking powder
- ½ tsp xanthan gum
- 30 g/1 oz ground almonds
- 55 g/2 oz vegan and gluten-free dark chocolate, chopped
- 125 ml/4 fl oz rapeseed oil
- 50 ml/2 fl oz gluten-free soya milk
- 50 ml/2 fl oz gluten-free soya cream
- 2 tbsp gluten-free raspberry jam
- chopped freeze-dried raspberries, to decorate (optional)

CHOCOLATE TOPPING

- 40 g/1½ oz vegan and gluten-free dark chocolate, broken into pieces
- 2 tbsp gluten-free soya cream
- ½ tsp vanilla extract

1 Preheat the oven to 180°C/350°F/Gas Mark 4. Line a 12-hole cupcake tin with paper cases. Make up the egg replacer in a small bowl according to the packet instructions and beat it with a fork for a minute until bubbly.

2 Put the sugar, glycerine and egg replacer into the bowl of a food mixer fitted with a whisk and beat on high speed for a minute. Alternatively, put the sugar, glycerine and egg replacer into a large mixing bowl and beat with a hand whisk or hand-held electric whisk until frothy.

3 Sieve the flour, baking powder and xanthan gum into the sugar mixture. Stir in the ground almonds and the chocolate.

4 Put the oil, soya milk and soya cream into a large jug and stir with a metal spoon. Pour over the flour mixture and mix thoroughly.

5 Put a little of the mixture into each paper case and use the back of a teaspoon to spread it out over the base. Put half a teaspoon of raspberry jam into each case, then divide the remaining cupcake mixture between the cases and smooth the tops with a spatula. Bake in the preheated oven for 20–25 minutes, or until springy to the touch and golden. Transfer to a wire rack to cool completely before icing.

6 To make the chocolate topping, place the chocolate into a heatproof bowl with the soya cream. Heat gently over a saucepan of gently simmering water to melt the chocolate. Stir frequently with a metal spoon to mix the chocolate and soya cream together. Stir in the vanilla extract. Take the bowl off the heat and beat the mixture with a metal fork until glossy and smooth. Decorate each cupcake with a thick layer of chocolate and a sprinkle of dried raspberries, if using. Set aside to cool and firm before serving.

Cook's tip

In order to maximize the pretty visual effect of these delicate cupcakes, be sure to bake these in dainty cupcake cases and not in larger, less attractive muffin cases.

Cook's tip

Many cake decorations contain egg or shellac which are not suitable for vegans. Dried blueberries make a pretty alternative topping for these cupcakes.

PREP TIME: 15–20 minutes COOK TIME: 20–25 minutes MAKES: 12

Blue Velvet CUPCAKES

Red velvet cupcakes often include beetroot – these unusual blue cakes contain ripe, buttery avocado for a rich, velvety texture.

½ ripe unwaxed avocado

225 ml/8 fl oz gluten-free soya milk

4 tsp vegan and gluten-free cider vinegar

5 tbsp rapeseed oil

1 tsp vanilla extract

1 tsp gluten-free blue food colouring paste

200 g/7 oz gluten-free self-raising flour

½ tsp xanthan gum

½ tsp gluten-free baking powder

200 g/7 oz caster sugar

FROSTING

70 g/2½ oz vegan and gluten-free margarine

70 g/2½ oz white vegetable shortening

600 g/1 lb 5 oz vegan and gluten-free icing sugar

4 tbsp gluten-free soya milk

¼–½ tsp gluten-free blue food colouring paste

1 Preheat the oven to 180°C/350°F/Gas Mark 4. Line a 12-hole mini muffin tin with paper cases.

2 Peel, stone and mash the avocado until smooth. Place the avocado in a large jug with the soya milk and vinegar, stir for a few seconds to combine the ingredients and set aside to curdle.

3 Put the oil, vanilla and food colouring paste into a small jug and stir with a fork to combine.

4 In a large bowl, sift the flour, xanthan gum and baking powder together and stir in the sugar with a wooden spoon.

5 Pour the soya milk mixture and the oil mixture onto the dry ingredients and stir well, to make sure the blue colouring is well dispersed. Over-stirring can result in rubbery cupcakes if you are using flour that contains gluten – but with this recipe, you can stir for as long as it takes to thoroughly combine the ingredients.

6 Divide the mixture evenly between the paper cases. Bake in the preheated oven for 20–25 minutes, or until cooked through and springy to the touch. Transfer to a wire rack and allow to cool completely before icing.

7 To make the frosting, beat the margarine and vegetable shortening together until soft and fluffy. An electric food mixer is easiest for this, but if you don't have one, put the margarine and shortening into a large mixing bowl and beat together with a fork until fluffy and well combined. Beat in the icing sugar and soya milk and as much blue food colouring as you need to achieve your desired effect. Pipe or spread the frosting generously with a palette knife onto the cupcakes.

PREP TIME: 20 minutes COOK TIME: 20–25 minutes MAKES: 10

Almond CUPCAKES

These simple almond cupcakes are enhanced by a delicious white chocolate icing.

- 5 tbsp rapeseed oil
- 4 tbsp gluten-free soya yogurt
- 160 ml/5½ fl oz gluten-free soya milk
- 160 g/5¾ oz caster sugar
- 3 tbsp almond extract
- 40 g/1½ oz ground almonds
- 160 g/5¾ oz gluten-free plain flour
- ½ tsp xanthan gum
- 1½ tsp gluten-free baking powder
- ½ tsp salt

ICING

- 60 g/2¼ oz vegan and gluten-free white chocolate, broken into pieces
- 100 g/3½ oz vegan and gluten-free icing sugar
- 1½ tbsp gluten-free soya milk
- toasted flaked almonds, to decorate

1 Preheat the oven to 180°C/350°F/Gas Mark 4. Line a cupcake tin with 10 paper cases.

2 Place the oil, yogurt, milk, sugar, almond extract and ground almonds in a large mixing bowl. Sift in the flour, xanthan gum, baking powder and salt then beat with an electric hand-held whisk until the mixture is well combined.

3 Divide the mixture between the cases in the prepared cupcake tin and bake in the preheated oven for 20–25 minutes, or until well risen and golden. Transfer the cupcakes to a wire rack and leave to cool completely before icing.

4 To make the icing, melt the chocolate in a large heatproof bowl set over a pan of simmering water. Remove from the heat and leave to cool slightly. Beat in the icing sugar and soya milk and spread the icing over the cupcakes with a teaspoon while the icing is still a little warm and easy to spread. Top each cupcake with a few toasted flaked almonds.

Cook's tip

If you would like these cupcakes to look more special, replace the flaked almonds with gold dragées.

2

3

4

PREP TIME: 25 minutes   COOK TIME: 20 minutes   MAKES: 12

Mojito CUPCAKES

These cupcakes are perfect for a hot summer afternoon – but take care as these are strictly for the grown-ups!

225 ml/8 fl oz gluten-free soya milk

2 sprigs fresh mint

1 tsp vegan and gluten-free cider vinegar

175 g/6 oz caster sugar

75 ml/2½ fl oz rapeseed oil

150 g/5½ oz gluten-free plain flour

2 tbsp gluten-free cornflour

½ tsp gluten-free bicarbonate of soda

½ tsp gluten-free baking powder

½ tsp salt

50 ml/2 fl oz vegan white rum

juice of 2 unwaxed limes

2 tbsp brown sugar

TOPPING

100 g/3½ oz vegan and gluten-free margarine

150 g/5½ oz white vegetable shortening

650 g/1 lb 7 oz vegan and gluten-free icing sugar

fresh unwaxed lime slices and fresh mint sprigs, to decorate

1 Put the soya milk into a small saucepan with the mint. Bring to the boil, then remove from the heat and leave to cool before removing the mint.

2 Preheat the oven to 180°C/350°F/Gas Mark 4. Line a 12-hole cupcake tin with paper cases.

3 Put the soya milk into a measuring jug, stir in the vinegar and set aside for a few minutes to curdle.

4 Put the sugar and oil into a large mixing bowl and beat together with a wooden spoon. Pour in the milk and vinegar and mix thoroughly. Add the flour, cornflour, bicarbonate of soda, baking powder and salt and mix together thoroughly.

5 Divide the mixture evenly between the paper cases. Bake in the preheated oven for 20 minutes, or until springy to the touch and golden.

6 Using a pastry brush, brush the tops of the cupcakes with some of the rum. Allow it to soak in and repeat two or three times. Brush with some of the lime juice and sprinkle each cake with a little brown sugar. Set aside the remaining rum and lime juice. Transfer the cupcakes to a wire rack to cool completely.

7 To make the topping, beat the margarine, white vegetable shortening and 500 g/1 lb 2 oz of the icing sugar together in a bowl until smooth. Beat in the remaining rum and lime juice. Gradually beat in additional icing sugar until the icing reaches a piping consistency. Pipe the icing generously onto the cupcakes and decorate each with a piece of lime and a fresh mint sprig.

Cook's tip

Mint teabags can also be used to infuse the soya milk in step 1.

Cook's tip

It is best to use a grater for the orange zest in the icing, but you could also use a zesting tool or a sharp knife to cut the decorative zest strips for these cake pops.

PREP TIME: 20 minutes, plus chilling

COOK TIME: 30 minutes

MAKES: 24

Chocolate Orange CAKE POPS

These fun, quirky-looking cake pops make a delicious contrast to traditional chocolate-covered cake pops.

1 chocolate brownie cake (see page 94), but made without macadamia nuts

24 lollipop sticks

ICING

25 g/1 oz vegan and gluten-free margarine

25 g/1 oz white vegetable shortening

225 g/8 oz vegan and gluten-free icing sugar

50 ml/2 fl oz gluten-free soya cream

TO DECORATE

250 g/9 oz vegan and gluten-free fondant icing sugar

juice and grated zest of 1 large unwaxed orange

zest from 1 large unwaxed orange, cut into strips

1 Make the brownie cake according to the recipe on page 94, but without the macadamia nuts. Leave to cool completely. Crumble the brownie into a large mixing bowl.

2 To make the icing, beat the margarine and shortening together with a wooden spoon. Mix in the icing sugar with sufficient soya cream to make an icing of a thick, spreadable consistency.

3 Add a little icing to the brownie crumbs and use your hands to mix it in. Gradually add more icing and use your hands to knead the mixture together. Continue to add icing until the mixture can be squeezed into small balls that hold together. Cover the bowl with clingfilm and refrigerate the mixture for 30 minutes.

4 Line a baking tray with baking paper. Roll the cake mixture into 24 small balls and place them on the prepared tray. Push a lollipop stick into each ball. Put the cake pops on the tray in the freezer for 30 minutes to firm up.

5 To decorate, mix the fondant icing sugar, orange juice and grated orange zest together in a medium-sized bowl. Take the cake pops out of the freezer and dip each one into the orange icing. Sprinkle with a few strips of orange zest. Return to the lined baking sheet and place in the freezer for 20 minutes until firm.

PREP TIME: 20 minutes, plus chilling

COOK TIME: 30 minutes

MAKES: 24

Chocolate Coconut CAKE POPS

These fashionable bite-sized treats are easy to make if you have a spare batch of brownies.

1 chocolate brownie cake (see page 94), but made without macadamia nuts

24 lollipop sticks

175 g/6 oz vegan and gluten-free dark chocolate, broken into pieces

55 g/2 oz desiccated coconut

ICING

25 g/1 oz vegan and gluten-free margarine

25 g/1 oz white vegetable shortening

225 g/8 oz vegan and gluten-free icing sugar

50 ml/2 fl oz gluten-free soya cream

1 Make the brownie cake according to the recipe on page 94, but without the macadamia nuts. Leave to cool completely. Crumble the brownie into a large mixing bowl.

2 To make the icing, beat the margarine and shortening together with a wooden spoon. Mix in the icing sugar with sufficient soya cream to make an icing of a thick, spreadable consistency.

3 Add a little icing to the brownie crumbs and use your hands to mix it in. Gradually add more icing and use your hands to knead the mixture together. Continue to add icing until the mixture can be squeezed into small balls that hold together. Cover the bowl with clingfilm and refrigerate the mixture for 30 minutes.

4 Line a baking tray with baking paper. Roll the cake mixture into 24 small balls and place them on the prepared tray. Push a lollipop stick into each ball. Put the cake pops on the tray in the freezer for 30 minutes to firm up.

5 Melt the chocolate in the microwave or in a heatproof bowl set over a saucepan of gently simmering water. Put the coconut into a shallow bowl. Dip each cake pop into the melted chocolate, then into the coconut, turning so that each cake pop is well covered. Place in a holder or on the lined baking tray to cool. Leave the chocolate to firm before serving.

Cook's tip

If you use your hands to mix the cake crumbs and the icing, rather than a spoon or mixer, then it's easier to tell when you have the right consistency to make the cake pops.

1

4

5

Cook's tip

You might like to add a very tiny drop of green food colouring to the peppermint cream filling, but it's best to keep the colour subtle rather than garishly green!

PREP TIME: 20 minutes COOK TIME: 10 minutes MAKES: 10

Chocolate & Peppermint WHOOPIE PIES

These little treats are devilishly moreish – you might find yourself making a second batch sooner than you think!

- vegan and gluten-free egg replacer, equivalent to 2 eggs
- 125 g/4½ oz vegan and gluten-free margarine
- 115 g/4 oz caster sugar
- 1 tsp vegan glycerine
- 115 g/4 oz gluten-free plain flour
- 1 tsp gluten-free baking powder
- ½ tsp gluten-free bicarbonate of soda
- ¼ tsp xanthan gum
- 30 g/1 oz vegan and gluten-free cocoa powder
- 5 tbsp gluten-free soya milk

FILLING

- 40 g/1½ oz vegan and gluten-free margarine
- 40 g/1½ oz white vegetable shortening
- 140 g/5 oz vegan and gluten-free icing sugar
- 2 tbsp gluten-free soya cream
- ½ tsp peppermint essence

1 Preheat the oven to 200°C/400°F/Gas Mark 6. Line two large baking trays with baking paper. Make up the egg replacer in a small bowl according to the packet instructions and beat it with a fork for a minute until bubbly.

2 Cream the margarine, sugar, egg replacer and glycerine together in a large bowl. Sift the remaining dry ingredients into the mixture, add the soya milk and quickly stir it all together.

3 Use two teaspoons to shape 20 small regular balls of the mixture and place them on the prepared baking trays. Bake in the preheated oven for 10 minutes, or until puffy and cooked through. Test with your finger – they should be soft but not sticky. Transfer to wire racks to cool.

4 To make the peppermint cream filling, beat the margarine, vegetable shortening, icing sugar, soya cream and peppermint essence together with a fork until smooth. Spread or pipe the filling onto the flat side of half of the bases, then sandwich together with the remaining cakes and serve.

PREP TIME: 15–20 minutes COOK TIME: 20–25 minutes MAKES: 12

Orange & Cinnamon MUFFINS

A surprise marmalade centre makes these sugar-topped cinnamon muffins a delicious treat for breakfast time.

175 g/6 oz gluten-free plain flour

1½ tsp gluten-free baking powder

½ tsp xanthan gum

40 g/1½ oz ground almonds

2 tsp ground cinnamon

zest of 1 unwaxed orange

175 g/6 oz granulated sugar

75 ml/2½ fl oz rapeseed oil

60 g/2¼ oz gluten-free soya yogurt

200 ml/7 fl oz gluten-free soya milk

4 tbsp gluten-free, unwaxed orange marmalade

TOPPING

4 tbsp brown sugar

1 tbsp ground cinnamon

1 Preheat the oven to 180°C/350°F/Gas Mark 4. Line a 12-hole muffin tin with paper cases.

2 Sift the flour, baking powder and xanthan gum into a large mixing bowl. Stir in the ground almonds, cinnamon, orange zest and sugar and mix well with a wooden spoon.

3 Mix the oil, yogurt and milk together in a large jug. Pour the wet mixture over the dry ingredients and stir with a wooden spatula until just combined.

4 Put 2 teaspoons of the mixture into the base of each paper case and use the back of the spoon to spread out the mixture, if necessary, so that the bases are completely covered. Put a teaspoon of marmalade into each muffin case. Divide the remaining muffin batter equally between the cases. Sprinkle each muffin with brown sugar and cinnamon.

5 Bake in the preheated oven for 20–25 minutes, or until the muffins are golden. Press the surface of one of the muffins with the back of a teaspoon to check whether it springs back. Transfer the muffins to a wire rack to cool (and to allow the sugar topping to become crisp) before serving.

Cook's tip

A sweet, fruity marmalade works well here but you could experiment with a tangy unwaxed Seville orange preserve or make a variation with unwaxed lemon marmalade.

2

3

4

Cook's tip

It is best to bake these muffins in the centre of the oven and not on the top shelf. This is so that the topping doesn't brown too quickly before the muffins are cooked in the centre.

PREP TIME: 20 minutes COOK TIME: 25–30 minutes MAKES: 12

Carrot & Pecan MUFFINS

These muffins are classic favourites and are enhanced by the added crunchy, spiced topping.

1 Preheat the oven to 180°C/350°F/Gas Mark 4. Line a 12-hole muffin tin with paper cases.

2 To make the topping, place the pecans in a small bowl. Stir in the sugar and mixed spice. Set aside.

3 Beat the sugar and oil together in a large mixing bowl, then stir in the flour, baking powder, xanthan gum and mixed spice and mix thoroughly. Add the carrots and pecans and stir with a wooden spoon until the mixture is well combined.

4 Divide the mixture equally between the muffin cases. Sprinkle the topping mixture over the muffins.

5 Bake in the preheated oven for 25–30 minutes, or until a skewer inserted into the centre of a muffin comes out clean. Transfer to a wire rack to cool.

225 g/8 oz brown sugar
175 ml/6 fl oz rapeseed oil
225 g/8 oz gluten-free self-raising flour
½ tsp gluten-free baking powder
½ tsp xanthan gum
½ tsp ground mixed spice
350 g/12 oz carrots, grated
200 g/7 oz pecan nuts, roughly chopped

TOPPING
85 g/3 oz pecan nuts, finely chopped
40 g/1½ oz brown sugar
½ tsp ground mixed spice

3

3

4

PREP TIME: 20 minutes COOK TIME: 25–30 minutes MAKES: 10

Mango & Coconut MUFFINS

These muffins have a taste of the Caribbean, with fresh, ripe mango and coconut flavours.

- 250 g/9 oz gluten-free plain flour
- 1 tbsp gluten-free baking powder
- 1 tbsp linseed meal
- 55 g/2 oz desiccated coconut, plus 2 tbsp for topping
- 125 g/4½ oz caster sugar
- 9 cardamom pods
- 175 ml/6 fl oz gluten-free soya milk
- 5 tbsp rapeseed oil
- 250 g/9 oz fresh, ripe unwaxed mango, chopped

1 Preheat the oven to 190°C/375°F/Gas Mark 5. Line a muffin tin with 10 paper cases.

2 Sift together the flour and baking powder into a large bowl. Mix in the linseed meal, coconut and sugar.

3 Crush the cardamom pods and remove the seeds. Discard the green pods. Crush the seeds finely in a pestle and mortar or with a rolling pin and stir into the mixture.

4 Whisk together the soya milk and oil in a small bowl and stir into the mixture, adding the mango at the same time. Mix until just combined; do not over-mix.

5 Divide the mixture between the 10 cases in the prepared muffin tin and sprinkle the top of each muffin with a little of the extra coconut. Bake in the preheated oven for 25–30 minutes, or until a skewer inserted into the centre of a muffin comes out clean. Leave to cool for 5 minutes before removing from the tin.

2

4

5

Cook's tip

For an alternative flavour, you could replace the mango with chopped unwaxed guava if you prefer.

PREP TIME: 20 minutes COOK TIME: 20–25 minutes MAKES: 12

Coffee & Walnut MUFFINS

These deliciously nutty muffins are a great choice for a breakfast on the go!

270 g/9½ oz gluten-free plain flour
1 tbsp gluten-free baking powder
2 tbsp gluten-free espresso powder
1 tsp ground cinnamon
175 g/6 oz caster sugar
250 ml/9 fl oz gluten-free soya milk
75 ml/2½ fl oz rapeseed oil
1 tbsp vanilla extract
100 g/3½ oz walnuts, chopped

TOPPING

30 g/1 oz walnuts, finely chopped
15 g/½ oz brown sugar

1 Preheat the oven to 180°C/350°F/Gas Mark 4. Line a 12-hole muffin tin with paper cases.

2 Sift together the flour, baking powder, espresso powder and cinnamon into a large bowl and stir in the caster sugar.

3 Whisk together the soya milk, oil and vanilla extract in a small bowl. Stir into the dry ingredients adding the chopped walnuts at the same time. Mix until just combined – do not over-mix.

4 Divide the mixture equally between the paper cases in the prepared muffin tin and sprinkle the top of each muffin with the finely chopped walnuts and brown sugar. Bake in the preheated oven for 20–25 minutes, or until a skewer inserted into a muffin comes out clean. Allow to cool slightly for 5 minutes before removing from the tin and serving.

2

3

4

PREP TIME: 20 minutes COOK TIME: 35–40 minutes MAKES: 12

Peach & Vanilla MUFFINS

Opinions are divided over whether muffins should ever be frosted, but the sticky peach glaze used here makes a delicious alternative.

- 3–4 ripe unwaxed peaches (approx. 450 g/1 lb), stoned
- juice of ½ unwaxed lemon
- 3 tbsp maple syrup
- 350 g/12 oz gluten-free plain flour
- 1 tsp gluten-free baking powder
- ½ tsp gluten-free bicarbonate of soda
- 1 tsp linseed meal
- 100 g/3½ oz brown sugar
- 125 ml/4 fl oz gluten-free soya milk
- 1 tbsp vegan and gluten-free white wine vinegar
- 1 tbsp vanilla extract
- 90 ml/3 fl oz rapeseed oil
- 70 g/2½ oz gluten-free, unwaxed peach preserve

1 Preheat the oven to 180°C/350°F/Gas Mark 4. Line a 12-hole muffin tin with paper cases.

2 Cut the peaches into eighths. Place in a shallow baking dish. Pour the lemon juice and maple syrup over the peaches and bake in the preheated oven for 15 minutes. Set aside to cool completely and leave the oven on.

3 Sift the flour, baking powder and bicarbonate of soda into a large mixing bowl. Stir in the linseed meal and sugar. Put the soya milk into a jug, stir in the vinegar and set aside for a few minutes to curdle.

4 Put half of the baked peaches and the juice from the baking tin into the bowl of a food processor. Add the vanilla extract and rapeseed oil and pulse the mixture to a purée. Roughly chop the remaining baked peaches.

5 Stir the milk mixture and peach purée into the dry ingredients, using a rubber spatula, until just combined. Fold in the chopped peaches.

6 Divide the mixture equally between the paper cases and bake in the preheated oven for 20–25 minutes, or until risen and springy to the touch. Transfer to a wire rack to cool.

7 To make the peach glaze, put the peach preserve into a small saucepan with 1 tablespoon of water. Bring to the boil, stirring continuously with a wooden spatula as you allow the mixture to boil vigorously for 1 minute. Remove the pan from the heat and continue to stir for a further 30 seconds. Brush the warm glaze over the muffins and allow to cool before serving.

Cook's tip

The baking powder and bicarbonate of soda begin to work as soon as you stir the wet ingredients into the dry ingredients, so work quickly to get these muffins into the oven.

PREP TIME: 20 minutes COOK TIME: 30 minutes MAKES: 12

White Chocolate BROWNIES

These chewy treats are also surprisingly packed with protein, thanks to the tofu in this recipe.

1 Preheat the oven to 160°C/325°F/Gas Mark 3. Line a 23-cm/9-inch square baking tin with baking paper so that the paper extends beyond the edge of the tin.

2 Put the tofu, milk and oil into the bowl of a food processor and process until smooth. Pour the mixture into a large mixing bowl and use a spatula to scrape the sides of the bowl.

3 Add the brown sugar, caster sugar and vanilla and beat together with a wooden spoon. Stir in the flour, xanthan gum, baking powder, bicarbonate of soda and salt and mix well. Fold the chocolate into the mixture.

4 Spoon the mixture into the prepared tin and use a spatula to push it into the corners and smooth the top. Bake in the centre of the preheated oven for 30 minutes, then remove from the oven – the texture will firm up as the brownies cool. Leave to cool in the tin for 10 minutes, then lift the baking paper and transfer the brownie, still on the paper, to a wire rack and leave to cool completely before slicing.

85 g/3 oz extra firm silken tofu
50 ml/2 fl oz gluten-free soya milk
50 ml/2 fl oz rapeseed oil
100 g/3½ oz brown sugar
100 g/3½ oz caster sugar
1 tsp vanilla extract
225 g/8 oz gluten-free plain flour
½ tsp xanthan gum
½ tsp gluten-free baking powder
½ tsp gluten-free bicarbonate of soda
¼ tsp salt
100 g/3½ oz vegan and gluten-free white chocolate, chopped into small pieces

Cook's tip

Brands of vegan white chocolate vary – some will melt, others bake to a toffee-like consistency, both of which can be good in brownies!

2

3

3

PREP TIME: 25 minutes   COOK TIME: 30 minutes   MAKES: 9

Chocolate & Macadamia BROWNIES

These rich and chocolatey brownies are a lovely mid-morning treat with a cup of tea or coffee.

- 2 tbsp linseed meal
- 225 g/8 oz gluten-free plain flour
- 1 tsp xanthan gum
- ¼ tsp gluten-free bicarbonate of soda
- 50 g/1¾ oz vegan and gluten-free cocoa powder
- 275 g/9¾ oz brown sugar
- 30 g/1 oz vegan and gluten-free dark chocolate
- 2 tsp vanilla extract
- ½ tsp vegan glycerine
- 85 g/3 oz vegan and gluten-free margarine, melted, plus extra for greasing
- 40 g/1½ oz macadamia nuts, roughly chopped

1 Preheat the oven to 180°C/350°F/Gas Mark 4. Grease and line a 20-cm/8-inch square baking tin with baking paper so that the paper extends beyond the edge of the tin.

2 Mix the linseed meal with 3 tablespoons of water and set aside for 10 minutes.

3 Sift together the flour, xanthan gum, bicarbonate of soda and cocoa powder in a large bowl. Add the sugar and combine thoroughly.

4 Break the chocolate into small pieces, place in a small bowl and pour over 4 tablespoons of boiling water. Stir thoroughly to melt the chocolate.

5 Stir the linseed paste, melted chocolate, vanilla extract, glycerine, melted margarine and chopped nuts into the dry ingredients. Use your hands to form the mixture into a soft dough. Press the dough into the prepared baking tin.

6 Bake in the preheated oven for 30 minutes, or until crisp around the edges but the centre is still soft. Carefully lift the brownie out of the tin using the lining paper, leave the paper on and place on a wire rack to cool for 10 minutes. Carefully peel away the paper and cut into nine squares. Leave to cool completely before serving.

CHAPTER 3

Cookies & Bars

PREP TIME: 20–30 minutes, plus chilling

COOK TIME: 10–12 minutes

MAKES: 12

Chocolate COOKIES

These are pretty enough to give away to friends as gifts and they are also fun for children to make.

- vegan and gluten-free egg replacer, equivalent to 1 egg
- 85 g/3 oz gluten-free plain flour
- 25 g/1 oz vegan and gluten-free cocoa powder
- ½ tsp gluten-free baking powder
- 25 g/1 oz vegan and gluten-free margarine
- 100 g/3½ oz caster sugar
- 55 g/2 oz vegan and gluten-free icing sugar

1 Make up the egg replacer in a small bowl according to the packet instructions and beat it with a fork for a minute until bubbly.

2 Sift the flour, cocoa and baking powder into the bowl of an electric food mixer (this is important to make sure the cookies are evenly coloured without any white flecks). Add the margarine and use your fingers to rub it in. When the mixture has a light, crumbly texture, add the caster sugar and egg replacer and beat together using the electric mixer. If you don't have an electric mixer, you can do this by hand with a wooden spoon but it may take several minutes for the mixture to come together to form a dough. When the mixture is clumping together, gather it into a ball, wrap it in clingfilm and place in the refrigerator to chill for 30 minutes.

3 Preheat the oven to 180°C/350°F/Gas Mark 4. Line a large baking sheet with baking paper.

4 Put the icing sugar onto a plate and spread it out. Use a sharp knife to divide the dough into 12 roughly equal pieces. Roll each piece into a small ball, and then gently roll the ball in the icing sugar until it is completely coated. Place the cookies on the prepared baking sheet, leaving a little space around each so that they can spread. Bake in the preheated oven for 10–12 minutes, then transfer the cookies to a wire rack to firm up. Leave to cool completely before serving.

Cook's tip

If you're cooking for adults, you could customize these treats by adding a splash of vegan amaretto or hazelnut liqueur to the mixture at the same time as the egg replacer.

3

4

5

PREP TIME: 25 minutes, plus freezing

COOK TIME: 15–20 minutes

MAKES: 12

Ice Cream SANDWICH COOKIES

These are a great treat when served straight from the freezer on a hot afternoon.

115 g/4 oz rice flour, plus extra for dusting

50 g/1¾ oz vegan and gluten-free cocoa powder

½ tsp gluten-free baking powder

pinch of salt

225 g/8 oz stoned, unwaxed dates, chopped

1 tsp vanilla extract

2 tbsp nut butter

5–6 tbsp almond or hazelnut milk

100–175 ml/3½–6 fl oz vegan and gluten-free ice cream, to serve

1 Preheat the oven to 150°C/300°F/Gas Mark 2. Cover a large baking sheet with baking paper.

2 Put the rice flour, cocoa powder, baking powder and salt into a large mixing bowl and mix well with a wooden spoon.

3 Place the dates in the bowl of a food processor with the vanilla extract, nut butter and 3 tablespoons of milk. Process to a creamy paste.

4 Stir the date paste into the flour mixture and gradually add up to 3 more tablespoons of milk. Use your hands to bring the mixture together to form a dough that is soft but not sticky.

5 Turn the dough out onto a lightly floured board and roll it to around 3 mm/⅛ inch thick. Use a 6-cm/2½-inch cookie cutter to cut out 24 cookies, re-rolling the dough trimmings as necessary.

6 Place the cookies on the prepared baking sheet. Bake in the preheated oven for 15–20 minutes, or until turning golden at the edges. Leave to cool a little on the baking sheet, then transfer the cookies to a wire rack to cool completely.

7 When the cookies are completely cool, take your ice cream out of the freezer and allow to defrost until it is just spoonable but not runny. Quickly sandwich two of the cookies together with 2–3 teaspoons of ice cream, then repeat to create 12 sandwiches in total. Return any unused ice cream to the freezer. Arrange the cookies on a baking sheet and freeze for at least an hour. Serve straight from the freezer.

Cook's tip

Almond or hazelnut milk or butter both work well in this recipe.

PREP TIME: 20 minutes, plus chilling

COOK TIME: 15 minutes

MAKES: 12

Lime FROSTED COOKIES

Everybody loves an iced cookie! Best eaten on the day they are made, these will be gone in no time.

- vegan and gluten-free egg replacer, equivalent to 1 egg
- 200 g/7 oz gluten-free plain flour, plus extra for dusting
- ½ tsp gluten-free baking powder
- pinch of salt
- 70 g/2½ oz vegan and gluten-free margarine
- 70 g/2½ oz golden caster sugar
- juice and zest of 1 unwaxed lime
- 1 tsp vegan glycerine
- 55 g/2 oz vegan and gluten-free fondant icing sugar
- strands of unwaxed lime zest, to decorate

1 Make up the egg replacer in a small bowl according to the packet instructions and beat it with a fork for a minute until bubbly.

2 Place the flour, baking powder and salt into a large mixing bowl. Add the margarine and rub it in with your fingers. Stir in the sugar. Add the lime zest, glycerine and egg replacer. Use your hands to work the mixture into a ball and transfer it to a lightly floured board. Knead the mixture and shape it into a log that is about 15 cm/6 inches long. Wrap it tightly in clingfilm and chill in the refrigerator for 1 hour.

3 Preheat the oven to 200°C/400°F/Gas Mark 6. Line a large baking sheet with baking paper.

4 Take the cookie dough out of the refrigerator, unwrap it and place on a lightly floured board. Using a serrated knife and a gentle sawing motion, slice the log into 12 cookies. Transfer the cookies to the prepared baking sheet.

5 Bake in the preheated oven for 15 minutes, or until just browning at the edges. Take care – they may brown underneath more quickly than they do on top. Take the cookies out of the oven and transfer immediately to a wire rack to cool completely.

6 Mix the lime juice with the fondant icing sugar. If your lime isn't very juicy, add a drop of water so that the icing is soft but not runny. Spread a little icing onto each cookie, decorate with a few pieces of lime zest and set aside to allow the icing to set before serving.

Cook's tip

A zesting tool will enable you to create long strands of zest that are perfect for decorating cakes. Vegan and gluten-free fondant icing sugar dries to a shiny finish which looks great on cookies.

2

4

6

Cook's tip

These cookies (without their filling) can be used in recipes that require gluten-free cookie crumbs to make biscuit bases, such as the Ice Cream Pie (page 148) in this book.

PREP TIME: 25 minutes COOK TIME: 15 minutes MAKES: 12

Peanut Butter SANDWICH COOKIES

These easy sandwich cookies are packed with protein from gluten-free oats and peanut butter – making them a great reward with a glass of chilled soya milk after an exercise session.

vegan and gluten-free egg replacer, equivalent to 1 egg

150 g/5½ oz gluten-free plain flour, plus extra for dusting

1 tsp gluten-free baking powder

115 g/4 oz gluten-free oats

115 g/4 oz brown sugar

125 g/4½ oz vegan and gluten-free margarine

115 g/4 oz crunchy peanut butter

FILLING

175 g/6 oz crunchy peanut butter

55 g/2 oz vegan and gluten-free icing sugar

55 g/2 oz vegan and gluten-free cocoa powder

55 g/2 oz vegan and gluten-free margarine

1 Preheat the oven to 180°C/350°F/Gas Mark 4. Line a large baking sheet with baking paper.

2 Make up the egg replacer in a small bowl according to the packet instructions and beat it with a fork for a minute until bubbly.

3 Sift the flour and baking powder into the bowl of an electric mixer. Add the oats, sugar, margarine, egg replacer and peanut butter. Beat together on a slow speed for 2 minutes, or until the mixture comes together in clumps. Alternatively, place the ingredients in a large mixing bowl and beat with a fork.

4 Turn the dough onto a floured board and pat it into a cylinder shape. Use a sharp knife to divide it into 12 equal pieces, then cut each piece in half again to form 24 pieces. Roll each piece of dough into a ball and place on the prepared baking sheet. Flatten each ball so that they are no more than 1 cm/½ inch thick.

5 Bake in the preheated oven for 15 minutes, or until just golden. Lift the baking paper to transfer the cookies to a wire rack and allow to firm up for 15 minutes before removing from the paper. Allow to cool completely before adding the filling.

6 To make the filling, beat the peanut butter, icing sugar, cocoa and margarine together until they are thoroughly combined and the mixture is smooth. The easiest way to do this is to put all the ingredients in a large mixing bowl and use a hand-held electric mixer, but you can also do it with a fork.

7 When the cookies are cool, spread half of them generously with the chocolate peanut butter filling and sandwich together with the remaining cookies.

PREP TIME: 15 minutes COOK TIME: 15 minutes MAKES: 14

Mocha COOKIES

These cookies have strong coffee and chocolate flavours and are great when accompanied by a vegan milky coffee or hot chocolate.

- 115 g/4 oz gluten-free plain flour
- ¼ tsp gluten-free baking powder
- 15 g/½ oz vegan and gluten-free cocoa powder
- 125 g/4½ oz brown sugar
- 1 tbsp gluten-free espresso powder
- 125 g/4½ oz vegan and gluten-free margarine
- 50 g/1¾ oz gluten-free porridge oats

1 Preheat the oven to 180°C/350°F/Gas Mark 4. Line a large baking sheet with baking paper.

2 Sift together the flour, baking powder and cocoa powder in a large mixing bowl. Add the sugar and combine thoroughly.

3 Dissolve the espresso powder in 1 tablespoon of boiling water and stir into the bowl. Add the margarine and oats and mix thoroughly to form a soft dough.

4 Form the mixture into 14 small balls, place on the prepared baking sheet and flatten slightly. Leave spaces between the cookies as they will expand during cooking. Bake in the preheated oven for 15 minutes, or until crisp. Transfer to a wire rack to cool, using a palette knife. Leave to cool completely before serving or storing in an airtight jar for up to 5 days.

2

3

4

PREP TIME: 10–15 minutes COOK TIME: 15 minutes MAKES: 12

Black Pepper SHORTBREAD

These crumbly shortbread biscuits have a warm peppery taste and are a perfect treat for a chilly day.

- 100 g/3½ oz rice flour
- 100 g/3½ oz gluten-free cornflour
- 85 g/3 oz caster sugar
- 125 g/4½ oz vegan and gluten-free margarine
- ½ tsp ground black pepper

1 Preheat the oven to 190°C/375°F/Gas Mark 5. Line a 25- x 18-cm/ 10- x 7-inch baking tin with baking paper.

2 Place all the ingredients into the bowl of an electric food mixer and mix on a slow speed until the ingredients are thoroughly combined. The mixture will develop a breadcrumb-like consistency after a minute and will start to clump together a few seconds later. Alternatively, place the sugar and margarine in a large mixing bowl and cream together with a fork until thoroughly combined. Add the rice flour, cornflour and black pepper, and mix with a wooden spoon until all the ingredients are thoroughly combined. The mixture will have a breadcrumb-like texture but should hold together when you pinch a little between your thumb and forefinger.

3 Transfer the mixture to the lined tin and press into an even layer. Use a sharp knife to mark the surface of the dough into 12 equal pieces. You can also use a fork to prick decorative patterns on the biscuits.

4 Bake in the preheated oven for 15 minutes, or until lightly golden. While the dough is still warm in the baking tin, cut it into pieces along the lines you made before baking. Leave to firm up in the tin before gently transferring to a wire rack to cool completely.

2

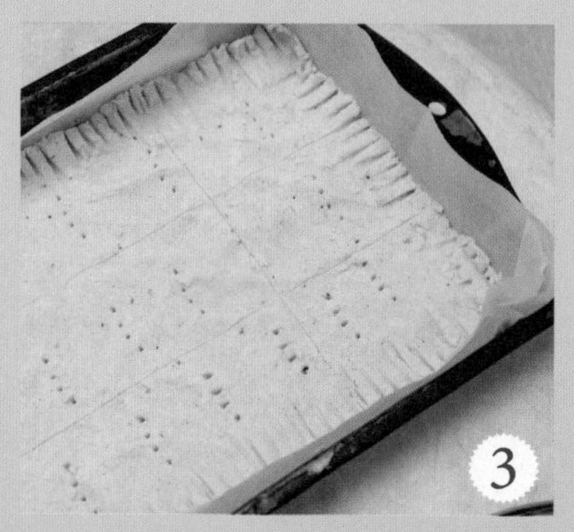
3

4

Cook's tip
Try using cinnamon in place of black pepper and serve with warm, baked unwaxed apples.

3

4

4

PREP TIME: 25 minutes COOK TIME: 40–45 minutes MAKES: 20

Salted Almond BISCOTTI

Chunky toasted almonds give these crunchy biscuits their traditional texture and a little sea salt adds a contemporary twist.

- 150 g/5½ oz whole almonds with skins
- vegan and gluten-free egg replacer, equivalent to 4 eggs
- 300 g/10½ oz gluten-free plain flour, plus extra for dusting
- 200 g/7 oz caster sugar
- ½ tsp gluten-free baking powder
- 1 tsp xanthan gum
- ½ tsp coarsely ground sea salt
- 1 tsp vanilla extract
- 150 g/5½ oz vegan and gluten-free dark chocolate, to decorate

1 Preheat the oven to 180°C/350°F/Gas Mark 4.

2 Put the almonds onto a large baking sheet and bake them in the preheated oven for 8 minutes, or until fragrant. Set aside to cool, then chop roughly. Line the baking sheet with baking paper. Make up the egg replacer in a small bowl according to the packet instructions and beat it with a fork for a minute until bubbly.

3 Put the flour, sugar, baking powder and xanthan gum into a large mixing bowl and mix thoroughly with a wooden spoon. Stir in the egg replacer, almonds, salt and vanilla. Use your hands to knead the mixture together to form a dough. Don't be tempted to add any water – it will come together.

4 Turn the mixture onto a floured board and cut into two pieces. Shape each piece into a flattened log around 30 cm/12 inches long. Transfer to the baking sheet and bake for 30–35 minutes, or until beginning to brown. Remove from the oven and carefully transfer to a chopping board. Using an oven glove to hold the hot dough, carefully slice each log diagonally into 10 slices. Lay the slices flat on the baking sheet and return to the oven for a further 10 minutes. Transfer to a wire rack to cool.

5 Break the chocolate into small pieces and melt in a microwave or in a heatproof bowl set over a pan of gently simmering water. Dip each biscotti into the chocolate and use a pastry brush to make sure each one is half coated. Place on a sheet of baking paper to dry.

Cook's tip

If you're cutting down on salt, replace it in this recipe with a tablespoon of unwaxed lemon or orange zest.

PREP TIME: 20 minutes, plus chilling

COOK TIME: 20–25 minutes

MAKES: 32

Earl Grey COOKIES

Serve these crisp cookies as an accompaniment to a fruit salad or compote – or with a nice cup of tea!

- 2 tbsp Earl Grey tea leaves
- 185 g/6½ oz gluten-free plain flour, plus extra for dusting
- 85 g/3 oz rice flour
- ½ tsp salt
- vegan and gluten-free egg replacer, equivalent to 1 egg
- 200 g/7 oz vegan and gluten-free margarine
- 100 g/3½ oz vegan and gluten-free icing sugar
- zest of 1 unwaxed lemon
- 100 g/3½ oz caster sugar

1 Chop the tea leaves very finely. If you have an electric coffee grinder or spice grinder, process the tea leaves to a fine powder. Put the tea into a large mixing bowl and stir in the flours and salt. Make up the egg replacer in a small bowl according to the packet instructions and beat it with a fork for a minute until bubbly.

2 Beat the margarine and icing sugar together until creamy. You can use a food mixer or do it by hand with a wooden spoon. Gradually incorporate the egg replacer and lemon zest. Stir in the flours, tea and salt and mix to a dough.

3 Turn the dough out onto a lightly floured board and gather it into a ball with your hands. Shape the dough into a log that is 30 cm/12 inches long and pat it into shape so that slices will be rectangular. Wrap it tightly in clingfilm and refrigerate for 1 hour.

4 Preheat the oven to 180°C/350°F/Gas Mark 4 and cover a large baking sheet with baking paper. Put the caster sugar into a small bowl.

5 Take the cookie dough out of the refrigerator, unwrap it and place it on a chopping board. Using a sharp serrated knife and a gentle sawing motion, cut the log into two equal pieces, then cut each piece into 16 slices. Dip each slice into the bowl of sugar, coating one side only. Place the cookies sugar-side up on the prepared baking sheet.

6 Bake in the preheated oven for 20–25 minutes, or until just golden. Leave the cookies to cool on the baking sheet for a few minutes, then use a palette knife to transfer them to a wire rack to cool completely.

Cook's tip

You can use the contents of two Earl Grey teabags in place of the loose tea – but be sure to use fresh teabags in order to achieve the best flavour for these cookies.

Cook's tip
It's important to turn the sheets during cooking so that the thin edges of the cookies do not burn.

PREP TIME: 20 minutes, plus chilling

COOK TIME: 15 minutes

MAKES: 24

Hazelnut THINS

With crispy, wavy edges and soft, chewy centres, these nutty cookies are everybody's favourites.

- vegan and gluten-free egg replacer, equivalent to 2 eggs
- 325 g/11½ oz gluten-free plain flour, plus extra for dusting
- 55 g/2 oz ground hazelnuts
- 1 tsp gluten-free bicarbonate of soda
- 1 tsp sea salt
- 225 g/8 oz vegan and gluten-free margarine
- 175 g/6 oz caster sugar
- 175 g/6 oz brown sugar
- 1 tsp vanilla extract

1 Make up the egg replacer in a small bowl according to the packet instructions and beat it with a fork for a minute until bubbly.

2 Put the flour, ground hazelnuts, bicarbonate of soda and salt into a large mixing bowl and stir together with a wooden spoon. In a separate bowl (or a food mixer), cream the margarine and sugars together with a wooden spoon, then beat in the egg replacer and vanilla with a whisk. Spoon the wet mixture into the dry mixture and mix thoroughly. Use your hands to bring the dough into a ball, wrap in clingfilm and chill in the refrigerator for 1 hour.

3 Preheat the oven to 180°C/350°F/Gas Mark 4. Line two large baking sheets with baking paper.

4 Take the cookie dough out of the refrigerator, unwrap it and place on a lightly floured board. Roll into 24 small balls and place them on the prepared baking sheets, leaving plenty of room for the cookies to spread as they bake.

5 Bake in the preheated oven for 15 minutes, rotating the sheets after 10 minutes. Leave the cookies to cool and firm for 5 minutes before lifting the baking paper onto wire racks. Leave the cookies to cool completely before taking them off the paper.

PREP TIME: 20 minutes, plus standing

COOK TIME: 40 minutes

MAKES: 18

Caramel Peach BARS

Juicy peach slices covered with sticky caramel sauce and a crunchy crumble base. These slices will be a very popular contribution to a coffee morning!

BASE

250 g/9 oz vegan and gluten-free margarine, plus extra for greasing

200 g/7 oz brown sugar

300 g/10½ oz gluten-free plain flour

200 g/7 oz gluten-free rolled oats

1 tsp gluten-free baking powder

TOPPING

55 g/2 oz gluten-free rolled oats

850 g/1 lb 14 oz canned unwaxed peach slices

150 g/5½ oz brown sugar

55 g/2 oz vegan and gluten-free margarine

3 tbsp gluten-free soya cream

½ tsp vanilla extract

1 Preheat the oven to 180°C/350°F/Gas Mark 4. Grease a 25- x 38-cm/ 10- x 15-inch baking tray and line with baking paper.

2 To make the base, put the margarine and sugar into a large mixing bowl and cream them together using a fork. Stir in the flour, oats and baking powder and knead together with your hands until it forms a sticky dough. Set aside 150 g/5½ oz of the mixture to use in the topping. Transfer the rest of the mixture to the prepared baking tray and press it into a smooth layer covering the base of the tin. Bake in the preheated oven for 20 minutes, then remove from the oven and set aside to cool. Leave the oven on.

3 To make the crumble topping, put the reserved mixture into a large mixing bowl and add the gluten-free oats. Use the tips of your fingers to rub the oats into the mixture. Scatter the mixture onto another baking tray and bake for 20 minutes, or until crisp and golden, then leave to cool.

4 Drain the peach slices then arrange them in overlapping rows over the cooled base.

5 To make the caramel topping, put the sugar, margarine and soya cream into a saucepan and heat gently, stirring constantly, to melt the ingredients together. Cook on a low heat for 5 minutes, or until the sugar has completely dissolved. Remove from the heat and stir in the vanilla. Spoon the warm caramel over the peaches. Avoid putting caramel at the edges of the baking tray as this can make it difficult to get the bars out of the tin. Sprinkle the crispy crumble topping over the caramel and set aside for around 30 minutes until the caramel has cooled completely.

6 Carefully lift the cooled mixture out of the baking tray, keeping the baking paper underneath it to support it, and place on a chopping board. Use a sharp knife to cut into 18 bars.

Cook's tip

Canned peach slices make an elegant and professional-looking topping for these bars, but you can use fresh peaches instead – you'll need around eight unwaxed peaches.

2

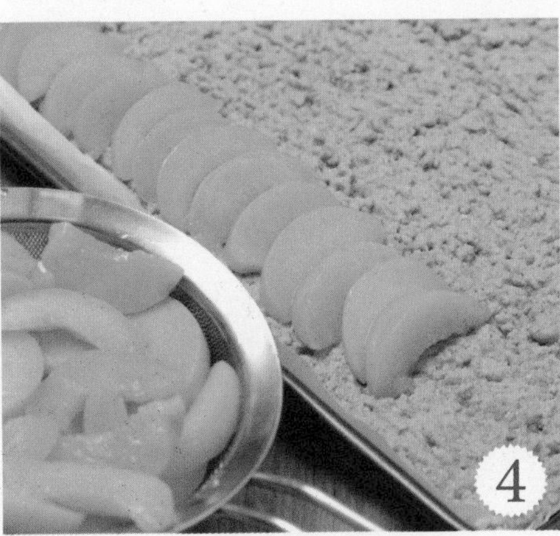
4

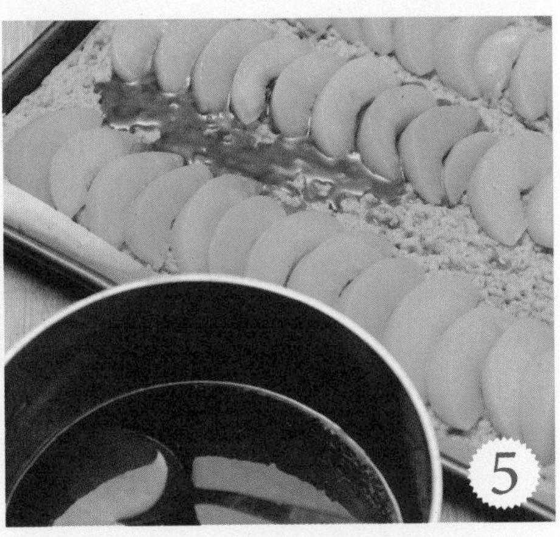
5

PREP TIME: 10 minutes, plus chilling

COOK TIME: 20 minutes

MAKES: 20

Coconut SQUARES

Traditionally coconut ice is made with condensed milk, but coconut cream makes a tasty alternative.

1 Line an 18-cm/7-inch square baking tin with clingfilm.

2 Put the coconut cream into a large saucepan with the sugar. Heat gently to melt the coconut cream and the sugar. Bring to boiling point and then simmer, stirring continuously, for 20 minutes to reduce the mixture to a thick syrup. If you have a sugar thermometer, check that the temperature is around jam-setting point (104°C/220°F). If you don't have a sugar thermometer, drop a little of the syrup onto a cold plate, wait for a minute and then carefully test it with your finger. It's ready when the surface wrinkles when you push the edge.

3 Stir in the coconut and cardamom powder, mix thoroughly with a wooden spoon and then spoon half of the mixture into the lined baking tin. Press down very firmly to form a smooth layer in the bottom of the tin. Mix the beetroot powder with 2 teaspoons of water and then mix it into the remaining coconut mixture. Make sure it is well distributed. Spoon the pink coconut into the tin and press it into a firm layer on top of the white coconut.

4 Put the coconut mixture into a refrigerator to chill for at least 4 hours, or overnight. Then turn it out of the tin and use a sharp knife to cut it into 20 squares.

225 ml/8 fl oz coconut cream

250 g/9 oz caster sugar

300 g/10½ oz desiccated coconut

1 tsp ground cardamom

¼ tsp beetroot powder

PREP TIME: 30 minutes COOK TIME: 25 minutes MAKES: 12

Lemon RIPPLE BARS

These soft lemony bars are a lovely teatime treat. Cut them into smaller squares for a dainty afternoon tea!

BASE

100 g/3½ oz gluten-free cornflour

100 g/3½ oz rice flour

85 g/3 oz caster sugar

125 g/4½ oz vegan and gluten-free margarine

FILLING

vegan and gluten-free egg replacer, equivalent to 3 eggs

115 g/4 oz vegan and gluten-free margarine

115 g/4 oz caster sugar

1 tsp vanilla extract

2 tbsp gluten-free plain flour

85 g/3 oz ground almonds

LEMON CURD

1 tsp gluten-free cornflour

juice of ½ unwaxed lemon

35 g/1¼ oz vegan and gluten-free margarine

40 g/1½ oz caster sugar

1 Preheat the oven to 180°C/350°F/Gas Mark 4. Line a 25- x 18-cm/10- x 7-inch baking tin with baking paper.

2 Place all the base ingredients into the bowl of an electric food mixer and mix on a slow speed until the ingredients are thoroughly combined. The mixture will develop a breadcrumb-like consistency after a minute and will start to clump together a few seconds later. Alternatively, place the margarine and sugar in a large mixing bowl and cream together with a fork until thoroughly combined. Add the rice flour and cornflour and mix with a wooden spoon until all the ingredients are thoroughly combined. The mixture will have a breadcrumb-like texture but should hold together when you pinch a little between your thumb and forefinger. Transfer the mixture to the prepared tin and press into an even layer.

3 To make the filling, make up the egg replacer in a small bowl according to the packet instructions and beat it with a fork for a minute until bubbly. Cream the margarine, sugar, egg replacer and vanilla extract together with a wooden spoon in a large mixing bowl. Mix in the flour and ground almonds. Spoon the mixture over the base and smooth the top with a spatula.

4 To make the lemon curd, put the cornflour into a small bowl and mix it to a paste with a little lemon juice. Put the rest of the lemon juice into a saucepan with the margarine and sugar, and heat gently, stirring, until the margarine has melted and the sugar has dissolved. Add the cornflour mixture and continue to cook for a further 2–3 minutes, or until the mixture has thickened but is still pourable. Drizzle 6–8 tablespoons of lemon curd over the filling. Use a knife to drag the lemon curd through the almond filling but don't overmix.

5 Bake in the preheated oven for 25 minutes, or until the almond filling is puffy and golden – the lemon curd will still be wet but will firm up as it cools. Leave to cool in the tin, then carefully lift out using the paper to support the base and cut into bars with a sharp knife.

Cook's tip
Line the base and sides of the tin with a single piece of baking paper and allow the paper to overhang the tin to make the bars easy to lift out after baking.

2

3

5

PREP TIME: 25–30 minutes, plus chilling

COOK TIME: 15–20 minutes

MAKES: 12

Rocky Road SLICES

A firm favourite with children and adults alike! Small portions are best for this sweet treat.

BASE

150 g/5½ oz vegan and gluten-free margarine, plus extra for greasing

70 g/2½ oz caster sugar

175 g/6 oz gluten-free plain flour

1 tsp xanthan gum

25g /1 oz vegan and gluten-free cocoa powder

TOPPING

350 g/12 oz vegan and gluten-free dark chocolate, broken into pieces

250 g/9 oz vegan and gluten-free margarine

1 tbsp golden syrup

125 g/4½ oz vegan marshmallows

100 g/3½ oz walnuts, roughly chopped

1 Preheat the oven to 180°C/350°F/Gas Mark 4. Grease a 20-x 30-cm/ 8- x 12-inch baking tray and line with baking paper.

2 To make the base, put the margarine and sugar into a large mixing bowl and cream them together using a fork. Stir in the flour, xanthan gum and cocoa and mix with a wooden spoon until the cocoa is well dispersed. Tip the mixture into the prepared baking tray and use the tips of your fingers to press into a smooth layer covering the base of the tin. Bake in the preheated oven for 15–20 minutes, then set aside to cool.

3 To make the topping, place the chocolate in a heatproof bowl set over a saucepan of simmering water. Add the margarine and golden syrup and melt the ingredients, stirring with a metal spoon until smooth. Set aside to cool a little.

4 If the marshmallows you are using are large, cut them into quarters or use baby marshmallows. Set half the marshmallows aside and stir the rest into the chocolate mixture along with the walnuts.

5 Pour the chocolate topping over the cooled biscuit base, spread it out with the back of a spoon and scatter the reserved marshmallows over the top. Refrigerate for 2 hours until firm, then use a sharp knife to cut into bars.

Cook's tip

Make sure you look for vegan marshmallows as ordinary marshmallows are not suitable for vegans.

PREP TIME: 10 minutes COOK TIME: 10–15 minutes MAKES: 16

Pistachio COOKIES

These are dainty cookies that contain no flour and can be made in under 25 minutes.

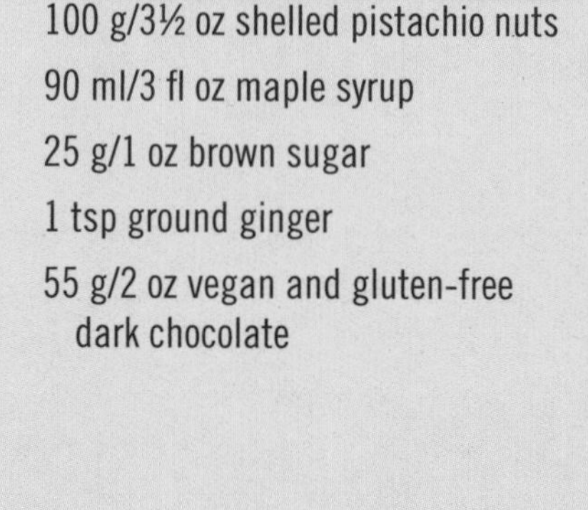

100 g/3½ oz shelled pistachio nuts
90 ml/3 fl oz maple syrup
25 g/1 oz brown sugar
1 tsp ground ginger
55 g/2 oz vegan and gluten-free dark chocolate

1 Preheat the oven to 180°C/350°F/Gas Mark 4. Line a large baking sheet with baking paper.

2 Put the pistachios into a heavy-based frying pan and roast them over a gentle heat, stirring constantly until they begin to brown. Tip them onto a plate and leave to cool completely.

3 Transfer the cooled pistachios to the bowl of a food processor fitted with a standard chopping blade. Add the maple syrup, sugar and ginger and process until the mixture begins to clump together. If you don't have a food processor, chop the pistachios very finely, put them into a large mixing bowl with the maple syrup, sugar and ginger, and mix with a metal spoon until completely combined into a sticky dough.

4 Tip the mixture onto a board, gently press into a thick sausage shape and cut it into 16 equal pieces. Roll each piece into a ball, place on the prepared baking sheet and flatten slightly. Bake in the preheated oven for 10–15 minutes, or until lightly browned. Lift the baking paper onto a wire rack and leave the cookies to cool and firm up.

5 Break the chocolate into small pieces and melt in a microwave or in a heatproof bowl, set over a saucepan of simmering water. Drizzle the liquid chocolate over the cookies and allow to cool completely.

Cook's tip
When the pistachios are roasting, be sure to tip them out as soon as they begin to brown to prevent them from burning.

Cook's tip
A handful of chopped almonds or walnuts would work well in these bars. Try substituting other dried fruits for some of the dates, too.

PREP TIME: 15–20 minutes COOK TIME: 15–20 minutes MAKES: 12

Coffee & Date SLICES

Brandy and espresso with sweet dates make a very tasty combination. Leave the brandy out if you're thinking of popping these into lunch boxes.

1 Preheat the oven to 180°C/350°F/Gas Mark 4. Line a 20- x 25-cm/ 8- x 10-inch baking tray with baking paper.

2 Put the dates into a small saucepan with 75 ml/2½ fl oz of water and the brandy, if using. Cook over a low heat for 2–3 minutes, or until the liquid has been absorbed, then remove from the heat.

3 Sift the flour and baking powder into a large mixing bowl. Stir in the almonds, linseed meal and espresso powder and mix well with a wooden spoon.

4 Stir the dates, maple syrup, date syrup and coconut oil into the dry ingredients and mix until thoroughly combined.

5 Transfer the mixture to the prepared baking tray and use your fingers to press into a smooth layer. Sprinkle the brown sugar over the top.

6 Bake in the preheated oven for 15–20 minutes, then remove from the oven and mark into 12 equal slices. Leave to cool completely in the tin, then re-cut along the marks and remove the slices piece by piece.

- 200 g/7 oz stoned, unwaxed dates, finely chopped
- 2 tbsp vegan brandy (optional)
- 70 g/2½ oz gluten-free self-raising flour
- 2 tsp gluten-free baking powder
- 70 g/2½ oz ground almonds
- 2 tbsp linseed meal
- 2 tbsp gluten-free espresso powder
- 2 tbsp maple syrup
- 1 tbsp unwaxed date syrup
- 2 tbsp coconut oil
- 3 tbsp brown sugar

PREP TIME: 20 minutes COOK TIME: 35–40 minutes MAKES: 12

Apricot & Raisin OAT BARS

Perfect if you're counting calories, these fibre-rich cereal bars contain almost no fat but have lots of flavour and are moist and chewy.

- 350 g/12 oz ready-to-eat dried unwaxed apricots
- 2 tbsp sunflower oil, plus extra for greasing
- finely grated rind of ½ unwaxed orange
- seeds from 5 cardamom pods, crushed (optional)
- 140 g/5 oz raisins
- 115 g/4 oz gluten-free rolled oats

1 Put the apricots into a saucepan with enough water to cover. Heat over a medium heat until almost boiling, then reduce the heat and simmer for 5 minutes, or until completely soft. Drain.

2 Put the apricots into a food processor with the sunflower oil and purée. Tip the purée into a bowl and stir in the orange rind and the cardamom seeds, if using. Leave to cool.

3 Preheat the oven to 180°C/350°F/Gas Mark 4. Brush a 20-cm/8-inch square baking tin with oil.

4 Stir the raisins and oats into the apricot mixture. Spread out the mixture in the prepared tin, levelling the surface with a spatula. Bake in the preheated oven for 35–40 minutes, or until firm. Cover with foil after about 25 minutes to prevent burning.

5 Leave to cool in the tin for 15 minutes. Turn out onto a wire rack and leave to cool completely before cutting into 12 bars.

Cook's tip

These cookies will keep for over a week in a sealed container so it's worth making a double batch!

1

4

4

PREP TIME: 15 minutes COOK TIME: 25 minutes MAKES: 12

Peanut Butter GRANOLA BARS

These crunchy peanut butter bars are good for a breakfast on the go or lunch-box snack.

1 Preheat the oven to 180°C/350°F/Gas Mark 4. Grease an 18- x 25-cm/ 7- x 10-inch shallow baking tin and line with baking paper. Cut the paper a little larger than necessary so that the edges are above the edges of the baking tin, as this will make it easier to lift the bars out.

2 Cream the peanut butter, sugar and golden syrup together. Using an electric food mixer is the easiest way to do this, but you can use a large mixing bowl and a wooden spoon. Stir in the granola and mix well. Put the mixture into the prepared tin and use the back of a metal spoon to press it into a smooth layer.

3 Bake in the preheated oven for 25 minutes, or until golden brown. Carefully lift the baked mixture out of the tin by holding the edges of the baking paper. Leave the baking paper underneath for support and place on a wire rack to cool completely. When the mixture is cool, use a sharp knife to cut into 12 bars.

- vegan and gluten-free margarine, for greasing
- 100 g/3½ oz crunchy peanut butter
- 30 g/1 oz brown sugar
- 2 tbsp golden syrup
- 450 g/1 lb gluten-free granola

PREP TIME: 20 minutes, plus chilling

COOK TIME: 5–7 minutes

MAKES: 12

Maple & Pecan GRANOLA BARS

The combination of maple and pecan is a classic flavour pairing and works really well in this tasty granola bar.

vegetable oil spray
165 g/5¾ oz gluten-free porridge oats
50 g/1¾ oz pecan nuts, chopped
50 g/1¾ oz flaked almonds
125 ml/4 fl oz maple syrup
50 g/1¾ oz soft light brown sugar
60 g/2¼ oz smooth peanut butter
1 tsp vanilla extract
¼ tsp salt
30 g/1 oz gluten-free puffed rice cereal
30 g/1 oz linseed meal

1 Preheat the oven to 180°C/350°F/Gas Mark 4. Coat a 23- x 33-cm/ 9- x 13-inch baking tin with vegetable oil spray.

2 On a large, rimmed baking tray, combine the oats, pecan nuts and almonds and toast in the preheated oven for 5–7 minutes or until lightly browned.

3 Meanwhile, combine the maple syrup, brown sugar and peanut butter in a small saucepan and bring to the boil over a medium heat. Cook, stirring, for about 4–5 minutes, or until the mixture thickens slightly. Stir in the vanilla extract and salt.

4 When the oats and nuts are toasted, place them in a mixing bowl and add the rice cereal and linseed meal. Add the syrup mixture to the oat mixture and stir to combine. Spread the syrup-oat mixture into the prepared baking tin and chill in the refrigerator for at least 1 hour before cutting into 12 bars. Serve at room temperature.

Cook's tip
If you prefer, you could swap
the pecan nuts for walnuts.
You could also try adding
some dried fruit!

CHAPTER 4

Desserts

PREP TIME: 40 minutes COOK TIME: 50 minutes SERVES: 8–12

Spiced Pumpkin PIE

A traditional-style pumpkin pie, flavoured with warming spices and maple syrup.

FILLING

450 g/1 lb pumpkin flesh, diced

350 g/12 oz firm silken tofu

125 ml/4 fl oz maple syrup

1 tsp vanilla extract

½ tsp ground cinnamon

½ tsp ground nutmeg

½ tsp ground ginger

½ tsp ground cloves

PASTRY

200 g/7 oz gluten-free plain flour, plus extra for dusting

25 g/1 oz rice flour

2 tbsp vegan and gluten-free icing sugar

½ tsp xanthan gum

pinch of salt

115 g/4 oz vegan and gluten-free margarine

vegan and gluten-free egg replacer, equivalent to 1 egg

1 To make the filling, steam the pumpkin for 25 minutes, or until tender. Leave to cool a little, then transfer to the bowl of a food processor with the remaining filling ingredients and process to a thick cream. Preheat the oven to 180°C/350°F/Gas Mark 4.

2 To make the pastry, put the flours, icing sugar, xanthan gum and salt into a large mixing bowl and mix together with a wooden spoon. Rub in the margarine with your fingertips. Make up the egg replacer in a small bowl according to the packet instructions and beat it with a fork for a minute until bubbly. Stir in the egg replacer and sufficient cold water to bring the mixture together to form a dough.

3 Turn the dough out onto a lightly floured work surface and shape into a firm ball. Roll the pastry out to around 3 mm/⅛ inch thick and use it to line a 23-cm/9-inch fluted baking tin.

4 Pour the filling into the pastry crust and smooth the top with a spatula. Bake in the preheated oven for 50 minutes. Leave the pie to cool in the tin for 10 minutes before serving or serve cold.

Cook's tip
The filling of this pie will still look soft when it comes out of the oven – but don't worry as the filling will firm up as it cools.

3

3

6

PREP TIME: 20 minutes, plus resting

COOK TIME: 45 minutes

SERVES: 6

Pecan & Cranberry PIE

This has the flavours of a classic dessert from the USA and is in the form of the traditionally American fruit pie!.

PASTRY

50 g/1¾ oz vegan and gluten-free margarine

150 g/5½ oz gluten-free plain flour, plus extra for dusting

½ tsp xanthan gum

15 g/½ oz vegan and gluten-free icing sugar

FILLING

30 g/1 oz dried cranberries

zest and juice of 1 unwaxed orange

1 tbsp vegan brandy (optional)

125 g/4½ oz pecan nuts

150 ml/5 fl oz maple syrup

100 ml/3½ fl oz gluten-free soya milk

3 tbsp vanilla extract

1 tsp ground cinnamon

1 tsp ground ginger

1 tsp linseed meal

1 Place the cranberries in a small bowl with the orange juice and brandy, if using. Set aside for at least an hour to plump up.

2 Preheat the oven to 190°C/375°F/Gas Mark 5.

3 To make the pastry, rub the margarine into the flour in a large mixing bowl and then stir in the xanthan gum and icing sugar. Gradually add sufficient cold water to make a soft dough. Roll the dough out on a floured work surface and use it to line a 20-cm/8-inch flan tin. Put the pecans into the pastry case and bake in the preheated oven for 15 minutes.

4 Put the maple syrup, soya milk, vanilla extract, cinnamon, ginger and orange rind into a medium saucepan over a low heat. Simmer gently for 5 minutes then remove from the heat.

5 Remove the pastry case from the oven but leave the oven on. Use a slotted spoon to remove the cranberries from the soaking liquid and arrange them on top of the pecans. Stir the linseed meal into the remaining soaking liquid and then stir this into the maple mixture.

6 Carefully pour the mixture into the pastry case. Return the pie to the oven for a further 30 minutes. Leave to cool before slicing and serving.

PREP TIME: 20 minutes, plus chilling

COOK TIME: 7–10 minutes

SERVES: 6

White Chocolate & Raspberry TARTLETS

These fresh and fruity raspberry tartlets with a smooth white chocolate filling are delicious and great for dinner parties.

PASTRY

- vegan and gluten-free egg replacer, equivalent to 2 eggs
- 150 g/5½ oz gluten-free plain flour, plus extra for dusting
- 30 g/1 oz vegan and gluten-free icing sugar
- 1½ tsp xanthan gum
- pinch of salt
- 85 g/3 oz vegan and gluten-free margarine

FILLING

- 55 g/2 oz vegan and gluten-free margarine
- 40 g/1½ oz caster sugar
- 1 tbsp gluten-free cornflour
- 325 ml/11 fl oz gluten-free soya milk
- 55 g/2 oz vegan and gluten-free white chocolate, broken into pieces
- 1 tsp vanilla extract

TOPPING

- 55 g/2 oz raspberries
- vegan and gluten-free icing sugar, for dusting (optional)

1 Preheat the oven to 180°C/350°F/Gas Mark 4.

2 To make the pastry, make up the egg replacer in a small bowl according to the packet instructions and beat it with a fork for a minute until bubbly. Put the flour, icing sugar, xanthan gum and salt into a large mixing bowl and mix together with a wooden spoon. Rub in the margarine with your fingertips. Stir in the egg replacer and use your hands to bring the mixture together in a soft ball.

3 Transfer the pastry to a lightly floured work surface and cut it into six equal pieces. Roll each piece out to line six shallow 10-cm/4-inch round, loose-based individual tartlet tins.

4 Bake the tartlet cases in the preheated oven for 7–10 minutes, or until just firm but not browning, then set aside to cool.

5 To make the filling, put the margarine and sugar into a small saucepan and heat gently, stirring, until the margarine has melted and the sugar has dissolved. Put the cornflour into a small bowl and mix to a smooth paste with a little of the soya milk. Add the chocolate to the saucepan with the remaining soya milk. Heat gently, stirring, until the chocolate has melted. Take the saucepan off the heat, add the cornflour paste and vanilla and beat with a whisk for 1 minute, or until the mixture is thick and smooth. Spoon the filling into the pastry cases and leave to cool, then transfer to a refrigerator and chill for 30 minutes.

6 Just before serving, cut the raspberries in half and arrange them on top of the tartlets. Dust with a little icing sugar, if desired.

2

3

5

Cook's tip
If you allow the filling to cool before using it, it will form a thick skin. If you make it in advance, cover it with clingfilm touching the surface until it is required.

PREP TIME: 20 minutes, plus chilling

COOK TIME: 15 minutes

SERVES: 6

Pear & Hazelnut TART

There are several steps to this recipe, but each one is quite easy and they add up to a very impressive tart.

DOUGH

150 g/5½ oz chopped toasted hazelnuts

25 g/1 oz brown sugar, plus 3 tbsp to serve

25 g/1 oz vegan and gluten-free margarine, plus extra for greasing

PEAR SLICES

2 tbsp caster sugar

1 large unwaxed pear

FILLING

40 g/1½ oz caster sugar

55 g/2 oz vegan and gluten-free margarine

40 g/1½ oz gluten-free cornflour

325 ml/11 fl oz gluten-free soya milk

1 tsp vanilla extract

1 Put the hazelnuts into the bowl of a food processor fitted with a chopping blade and process until finely chopped. Add the brown sugar and margarine and process for a further minute until the mixture comes together as a soft dough. Form the dough into a ball, wrap with clingfilm and put into the refrigerator to chill for at least 30 minutes.

2 Preheat the oven to 150°C/300°F/Gas Mark 2. Grease an 18-cm/7-inch springform cake tin. Put the caster sugar into a large saucepan with 3 tablespoons of water and heat it gently, stirring occasionally, for 1 minute, or until the sugar has dissolved and the liquid is clear. Slice the pear in half from top to bottom, then cut each half lengthways into three slices of equal thickness. Arrange the pear slices in the saucepan and increase the heat so that the sugar syrup bubbles gently. Cook the pears in the syrup, turning occasionally, for 5 minutes, or until the pear is soft and the syrup is very reduced and sticky. Leave the pears in the saucepan to cool.

3 Take the hazelnut dough out of the refrigerator and use your fingers to press it into the prepared tin. Press the mixture down firmly and make sure the base is covered. Bring the mixture up the sides of the tin to form a pie crust about 4 cm/1½ inches deep. Bake in the preheated oven for 15 minutes, then set aside to cool.

4 To make the filling, put the caster sugar and margarine into a large saucepan. Heat gently to melt the margarine. Put the cornflour into a small bowl and add sufficient soya milk to make a smooth paste. Pour the rest of the soya milk into the saucepan and bring to boiling point. Reduce the heat to low and whisk in the cornflour mixture and vanilla. Keep whisking until the mixture thickens – this will take about 3 minutes. The consistency should be like a very thick custard (too thick to pour). Allow the filling to cool for 5 minutes, then carefully spoon it into the hazelnut crust and smooth the surface with a spatula. Carefully arrange the pear slices on top, pressing them down gently so that the surface of the pears is at the same level as the surface of the filling. Chill then serve with a sprinkle of brown sugar.

PREP TIME: 35 minutes   COOK TIME: 35–40 minutes   SERVES: 10

Plum FRANGIPANE

This is a large, decorative tart that is ideal for entertaining or for serving for family dinners.

1 Preheat the oven to 180°C/350°F/Gas Mark 4. Make up the egg replacers for the pastry and the filling in two small bowls according to the packet instructions and beat them with a fork for a minute until bubbly.

2 To make the pastry, put the flour, icing sugar, xanthan gum and salt into a large mixing bowl and mix together with a wooden spoon. Rub in the margarine with your fingertips. Stir in the egg replacer and sufficient cold water to bring the mixture together to form a dough.

3 Turn the dough onto a lightly floured work surface and shape it into a firm ball. Roll the pastry out to around 3 mm/⅛ inch thick and use it to line a 25-cm/10-inch round, fluted baking tin. Bake the pastry shell for 10 minutes, then set aside to cool.

4 To make the filling, cream the margarine, sugar, egg replacer, amaretto and vanilla extract together with a wooden spoon in a large mixing bowl. Mix in the flour and ground almonds.

5 Spoon the filling into the pastry shell and smooth the top with a spatula. Bake in the preheated oven for 25–30 minutes, or until the top is golden. Set aside to cool and firm.

6 Put the apricot jam into a small saucepan with a tablespoon of water. Bring to the boil, stirring constantly, then pass through a fine sieve and leave to cool a little. Arrange the plums on top of the tart and pour the jam glaze over the top. Leave to cool slightly before serving.

PASTRY

vegan and gluten-free egg replacer, equivalent to 2 eggs

150 g/5½ oz gluten-free plain flour, plus extra for dusting

30 g/1 oz vegan and gluten-free icing sugar

1½ tsp xanthan gum

pinch of salt

85 g/3 oz vegan and gluten-free margarine

FILLING

vegan and gluten-free egg replacer, equivalent to 3 eggs

115 g/4 oz vegan and gluten-free margarine

115 g/4 oz caster sugar

1 tbsp vegan amaretto

1 tsp vanilla extract

2 tbsp gluten-free plain flour

85 g/3 oz ground almonds

TOPPING

175 g/6 oz gluten-free, unwaxed apricot jam

400 g/14 oz unwaxed red-skinned plums, stoned and sliced

2

3

5

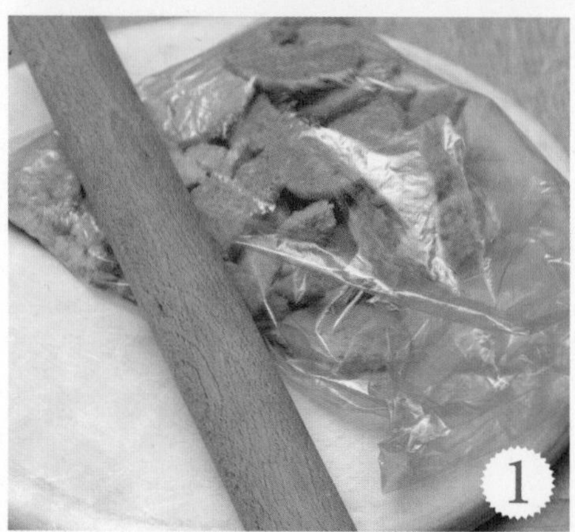
1

2

4

PREP TIME: 25 minutes, plus freezing

COOK TIME: None

SERVES: 12

Ginger Ice Cream PIE

Chopped stem ginger adds some sophistication to a pie that's real comfort food.

- 300 g/10½ oz vegan and gluten-free ginger biscuits
- 2 tbsp coconut oil
- 2 tbsp maple syrup
- 1 tbsp ginger syrup from a jar of preserved stem ginger
- 100 g/3½ oz vegan and gluten-free chocolate nut spread
- 750 ml/1¼ pints vegan and gluten-free vanilla ice cream
- 30 g/1 oz preserved stem ginger, finely chopped

1 Crush the biscuits to fine crumbs using a food processor or put them into a sealed plastic food bag, lay the bag on a chopping board and break up the biscuits with a rolling pin. Set aside 3 tablespoons of the crushed biscuits to use as the topping for the pie.

2 Put the rest of the crushed biscuits into a large mixing bowl with the coconut oil, maple syrup and ginger syrup, and stir together with a wooden spoon until well combined.

3 Pour the biscuit mixture into a 20-cm/8-inch round, loose-based cake tin. Use the tips of your fingers to press it into a smooth layer covering the base of the tin.

4 Warm the chocolate nut spread a little, either in a small bowl in the microwave or in a small saucepan on the hob, so that it softens and becomes easier to spread. Carefully spoon it into the tin and use the back of a spoon or a rubber spatula to spread it over the crumb base.

5 Place the crumb base in the freezer for at least an hour to firm.

6 Take the ice cream out of the freezer and allow it to soften at room temperature for about 15 minutes, or until it is soft enough to mash but not completely runny. Put the softened ice cream into a large mixing bowl. Stir the stem ginger into the ice cream, making sure it is well dispersed.

7 Take the crumb base out of the freezer and fill it with the ice cream. Smooth the top and sprinkle over the reserved crushed ginger biscuits. Return to the freezer for at least an hour before serving. To serve, lift the pie out of the tin, place on a plate and allow to soften at room temperature for a few minutes before cutting into slices.

Cook's tip

The layer of chocolate spread can be omitted if you can't obtain this ingredient – or use a thin layer of melted vegan and gluten-free dark chocolate instead.

PREP TIME: 20 minutes, plus soaking

COOK TIME: None

SERVES: 8

Raw Fruit TART

This quick and easy fruit tart is a guilt-free treat – try it for breakfast!

1 Soak the cashews for the cashew cream in a bowl of water for approximately 8 hours or overnight.

2 Put all the ingredients for the tart base into the bowl of a food processor fitted with a chopping blade. Process until the nuts are finely chopped and the mixture begins to clump together. Press the mixture into the base of a 20-cm/8-inch pie dish and use the back of a spoon to smooth it into a firm crust.

3 To make the mixed fruit topping, you might like to halve strawberries, grapes or blackberries, and core and chop apples or pears. Put the prepared fruit into a large mixing bowl and toss with the lemon juice and vanilla extract. Arrange the fruit over the tart base.

4 To make the cashew cream, drain the soaked cashews and put them into the bowl of a food processor fitted with a chopping blade. Add the agave nectar, lemon juice and 175 ml/6 fl oz of cold water. Blend to a smooth cream and serve immediately with the tart.

BASE

150 g/5½ oz pecan nuts

55 g/2 oz stoned, unwaxed dates

1 tsp ground cinnamon

1 tbsp vanilla extract

a pinch of salt

TOPPING

280 g/10 oz mixed fresh unwaxed fruit (choose a colourful selection of fresh fruit in season)

juice of ½ an unwaxed lemon

1 tbsp vanilla extract

CASHEW CREAM

225 g/8 oz cashew nuts

1 tbsp agave nectar

1 tbsp unwaxed lemon juice

Cook's tip

Soaking the cashews makes the cashew cream less grainy but, if time is short, you can skip the soaking and it will still work well.

1

3

4

PREP TIME: 30 minutes COOK TIME: 20 minutes SERVES: 6

Rhubarb & Custard TARTLETS

Rhubarb and custard is a retro combination that's back in fashion – a delectable mixture of sweet and creamy with tart and tangy!

140 g/5 oz fresh rhubarb, chopped

30 g/1 oz caster sugar

450 ml/16 fl oz custard (made with vegan and gluten-free custard powder and soya milk)

PASTRY

vegan and gluten-free egg replacer, equivalent to 2 eggs

150 g/5½ oz gluten-free plain flour, plus extra for dusting

30 g/1 oz vegan and gluten-free icing sugar

1½ tsp xanthan gum

85 g/3 oz vegan and gluten-free margarine

1 Place the rhubarb into a small saucepan with the sugar and 3 tablespoons of water. Cook over a medium heat for 3–4 minutes, stirring frequently, until the rhubarb has disintegrated. Set aside to cool.

2 Make up the custard following the instructions on the custard powder packet. Set aside to cool. Make up the egg replacer in a small bowl according to the packet instructions and beat it with a fork for a minute until bubbly. Preheat the oven to 160°C/325°F/Gas Mark 3.

3 To make the pastry, put the flour, icing sugar and xanthan gum into a large mixing bowl and stir with a wooden spoon to combine. Rub in the margarine with your fingertips, then gradually stir in the egg replacer and use your hands to bring the mixture together in a soft ball.

4 Transfer the pastry to a lightly floured work surface and cut it into six equal pieces. Roll each piece out to line six shallow 10-cm/4-inch round, loose-based individual tartlet tins.

5 Bake the tartlet cases in the preheated oven for 7–10 minutes, or until just firm but not browning, then remove from the oven and fill with the cooled custard. Swirl two or three teaspoons of rhubarb into each tartlet.

6 Return the tartlets to the oven and bake for 10 more minutes, or until the custard is just golden. Serve warm or cold.

Cook's tip

You can buy ready-made vegan custard, but it's best to start from scratch with custard powder as the ready-made custard does not set as well in the tartlets.

PREP TIME: 30 minutes, plus chilling

COOK TIME: 15 minutes

SERVES: 8

Chocolate & Banana CREAM PIE

With bananas, cashews and chocolate all used in this recipe, it makes a great showcase for a range of tasty ingredients!

CRUST

150 g/5½ oz cashew nuts

25 g/1 oz brown sugar

25 g/1 oz vegan and gluten-free cocoa powder

25 g/1 oz vegan and gluten-free margarine, plus extra for greasing

BANANA CREAM

125 g/4½ oz cashew nuts

350 g/12 oz extra firm silken tofu

100 g/3½ oz caster sugar

2 tbsp unwaxed lemon juice

2 tbsp coconut oil

2 very ripe unwaxed bananas (about 175 g/6 oz)

pinch of salt

CHOCOLATE GANACHE

40 g/1½ oz vegan and gluten-free dark chocolate, broken into pieces

2 tbsp coconut milk

½ tsp vanilla extract

dried vegan banana chips, to decorate (optional)

1 Grease an 18-cm/7-inch springform cake tin.

2 To make the crust, put the cashews into a heavy-based frying pan and heat them gently, stirring frequently, for 2–3 minutes, or until they begin to turn golden. Leave to cool then transfer to the bowl of a food processor fitted with a chopping blade and process until very finely chopped. Add the sugar, cocoa powder and margarine and process for a further minute until the mixture comes together as a soft dough. Form the dough into a ball, wrap it with clingfilm and place in the refrigerator to chill for at least 30 minutes. Preheat the oven to 150°C/300°F/Gas Mark 2.

3 Take the cashew crust out of the refrigerator and use your fingers to press it into the prepared tin. Press the mixture down firmly. Bring the mixture up the sides of the tin to form a pie crust about 4 cm/1½ inches deep. Bake in the preheated oven for 15 minutes, then set aside to cool.

4 To make the banana cream, put the cashews into the bowl of a food processor fitted with a chopping blade and process to a fine powder. Add the remaining ingredients and process to a smooth, thick cream. Spoon the banana cream into the pie crust, smooth the top and refrigerate for at least an hour.

5 To make the chocolate topping, place the chocolate in a heatproof bowl with the coconut milk. Place over a saucepan of gently simmering water and stir frequently with a metal spoon to melt together. Stir in the vanilla extract. Take the bowl off the heat and beat the mixture with a metal fork until glossy and smooth.

6 Take the pie out of the refrigerator, spoon the warm chocolate mixture over the top, quickly smooth it with a rubber spatula and decorate with banana chips, if using. Return the pie to the refrigerator to chill for at least another hour before loosening the sides of the tin and transferring to a plate to serve.

Cook's tip

Don't be tempted to cut back on the chilling time in this recipe as you need to fully chill the pie in order to be sure that it holds its shape when it is sliced.

1

3

4

PREP TIME: 35 minutes COOK TIME: 30 minutes SERVES: 8

Apple & Cinnamon PIE

An autumn or winter classic, this is a generous showstopper dessert to finish off any family meal or dinner party.

1 To make the pastry, put the vegetable shortening and margarine into a large mixing bowl. Pour over 100 ml/3½ fl oz of boiling water and mix with a wooden spoon until creamy. Add the flour, baking powder and salt, stir together, then turn out onto a lightly floured work surface and knead together into a smooth ball. Leave the dough to cool for 5 minutes. Roll the dough out on a sheet of clingfilm to a shape that slightly overhangs a 23-cm/9-inch round pie dish. Set aside.

2 Preheat the oven to 180°C/350°F/Gas Mark 4.

3 Place the apples in a large saucepan with the sugar, cornflour and cinnamon, and add 3 tablespoons of water. Cook gently for 5–10 minutes, or until the apple is just tender and most of the liquid in the pan has been thickened by the cornflour. Leave the mixture to cool.

4 Put the apple filling into the pie dish. Lift the pastry on the sheet of clingfilm (to support it) and carefully transfer the pastry to the top of the pie, pressing the edges down to form a crust and trimming away any excess with a sharp knife. Re-roll the trimmings to make decorative leaves and place these on top of the pie.

5 Brush the top of the pie with a little soya milk and sprinkle with a little caster sugar. Bake in the preheated oven for 30 minutes, or until just golden. Serve hot or cold.

PASTRY

- 60 g/2¼ oz white vegetable shortening
- 15 g/½ oz vegan and gluten-free margarine
- 225 g/8 oz gluten-free plain flour, plus extra for dusting
- 1 tbsp gluten-free baking powder
- pinch of salt
- gluten-free soya milk, for brushing
- caster sugar, for sprinkling

FILLING

- 1 kg/2 lb 4 oz unwaxed cooking apples, peeled, cored and sliced
- 150 g/5½ oz caster sugar
- 2 tsp gluten-free cornflour
- 1 tbsp ground cinnamon

Cook's tip

Precooking the apples removes some of the water that could otherwise make the pastry soggy.

PREP TIME: 20 minutes, plus chilling

COOK TIME: 40 minutes

SERVES: 8

Mango CHEESECAKE

This is a rich dessert, but lightened by the fresh flavour of the sliced mango topping and filling.

- 70 g/2½ oz vegan and gluten-free margarine, plus extra for greasing
- 175 g/6 oz vegan and gluten-free biscuits, crushed
- 40 g/1½ oz ground almonds

FILLING

- 1 large unwaxed mango, stoned, peeled and diced
- juice of 1 unwaxed lemon
- 200 g/7 oz gluten-free soya yogurt
- 1 tbsp gluten-free cornflour
- 3 tbsp maple syrup
- 450 g/1 lb vegan and gluten-free cream cheese

TOPPING

- 3 tbsp maple syrup
- 1 small unwaxed mango, stoned, peeled and sliced

1 Preheat the oven to 180°C/350°F/Gas Mark 4. Lightly grease a 23-cm/9-inch round, loose-bottomed cake tin.

2 To make the biscuit base, melt the margarine in a saucepan, then stir in the crushed biscuits and almonds with a wooden spoon. Press the mixture into the base of the prepared cake tin to make an even layer. Bake in the preheated oven for 10 minutes.

3 Meanwhile, to make the filling, put the mango, lemon juice, yogurt, cornflour, maple syrup and cream cheese into a food processor or blender and process until smooth. Pour the mixture over the biscuit base and smooth the surface.

4 Bake for 25–30 minutes, or until golden and set. Leave to cool in the tin, then transfer to a wire rack and chill in the refrigerator for 30 minutes.

5 To make the topping, heat the maple syrup in a saucepan. Brush the top of the cheesecake with some of the maple syrup. Add the mango to the remaining maple syrup in the pan and cook for 1 minute, stirring. Leave to cool slightly, then arrange the mango slices on top of the cheesecake. Pour over any remaining syrup before serving.

Cook's tip

This cheesecake also tastes great with fresh unwaxed passion fruit drizzled over the top.

Cook's tip
Acidic fruit will melt vegan jellies, so decorate your cheesecake with a little grated dark chocolate instead.

PREP TIME: 25 minutes, plus chilling

COOK TIME: None

SERVES: 8

Lemon Jelly CHEESECAKE

This is an unusual but delicious cheesecake, with a crispy rice base and smooth lemony topping.

30 g/1 oz gluten-free rice cakes

85 g/3 oz vegan and gluten-free dark chocolate, broken into pieces, plus extra grated chocolate to decorate (optional)

30 g/1 oz vegan hazelnut butter

TOPPING

85 g/3 oz vegan and gluten-free lemon jelly crystals

350 g/12 oz vegan and gluten-free cream cheese

1 Line a 20-cm/8-inch round, springform baking tin with kitchen foil, letting the foil extend beyond the edges of the tin.

2 Crush or chop the rice cakes into fine pieces, or process them briefly in a food processor so that they still have some texture. Melt the chocolate and hazelnut butter together in a heatproof bowl set over a small saucepan of gently simmering water. Put the crushed rice cakes into a large mixing bowl, pour in the chocolate mixture and stir until all the rice pieces are coated with chocolate.

3 Put the mixture into the prepared tin and press it down with the back of a spoon. Chill in the refrigerator for 30 minutes, until the chocolate has set.

4 Follow the instructions on the jelly packet to make 600 ml/1 pint of lemon jelly. Leave the mixture in a large measuring jug to cool but not set. When the mixture is cool, pour it into the bowl of a food processor, add the cream cheese and process until smooth.

5 Pour the jelly mixture over the top of the rice base. Put the cheesecake back into the refrigerator for 2 hours, or until completely set. To serve, carefully release the sides of the tin and use the foil for support as you transfer it to a serving plate. Decorate with grated chocolate, if desired.

PREP TIME: 20 minutes, plus chilling

COOK TIME: 2 hours

SERVES: 8

Pear & Cardamom CHEESECAKE

The base of this cheesecake is made with crushed rice cakes, which gives it a wonderfully crispy and chewy texture.

BASE

vegan and gluten-free margarine, for greasing

40 g/1½ oz stoned, unwaxed dates, chopped

2 tsp coconut oil

30 g/1 oz gluten-free rice cakes

40 g/1½ oz desiccated coconut

FILLING

350 g/12 oz extra firm silken tofu

225 g/8 oz vegan and gluten-free cream cheese

30 g/1 oz caster sugar

30 g/1 oz gluten-free plain flour

¼ tsp xanthan gum

1 tsp ground cardamom

pinch of salt

¼ tsp gluten-free bicarbonate of soda

2 unwaxed pears, peeled, cored and finely chopped

PEAR CRISPS

25 g/1 oz caster sugar

1 tbsp unwaxed lemon juice

1 unwaxed pear, sliced vertically into very thin slices

1 Preheat the oven to 180°C/350°F/Gas Mark 4. Grease a 20-cm/8-inch springform cake tin and line with baking paper.

2 Put the dates into a small saucepan with 90 ml/3 fl oz water over a low heat. Heat gently and simmer for 5 minutes, or until they are softening into the water. Stir in the coconut oil and melt the oil into the date mixture. Crush the rice cakes finely – a food processor is best for this but you could also use a rolling pin. Stir the crushed rice cakes and desiccated coconut into the date mixture and mix together thoroughly.

3 Spoon the crust mixture into the prepared tin and use the back of a metal spoon to press it down firmly, making a smooth layer to cover the base of the tin.

4 To make the filling, put all the ingredients, except the pears, into the bowl of a food processor fitted with a chopping blade and process until smooth and creamy. Fold the pears into the mixture. Spoon the filling into the tin and smooth the top with a rubber spatula. Bake in the preheated oven for 45–50 minutes, or until beginning to brown. The cheesecake should still be wobbly when you take it out of the oven. Leave to cool at room temperature and then put it into the refrigerator for at least 2 hours to chill and set.

5 To make the pear crisps, preheat the oven to 140°C/275°F/Gas Mark 1. Put the sugar and lemon juice into a small saucepan with 1 tablespoon of water and warm gently to dissolve the sugar. Take the pan off the heat and carefully dip each pear slice into the sugar solution, then place the slices on a baking tray lined with baking paper. Bake in the preheated oven for 1 hour, or until crisp and golden, then carefully transfer to a clean sheet of baking paper to cool. Decorate the cheesecake with pear crisps just before serving.

2

3

5

PREP TIME: 20 minutes COOK TIME: 45–55 minutes SERVES: 6

Rhubarb & Blackberry CRUMBLE

This is a classic winter warmer that is so comforting that it banishes away the cold weather blues!

1 Preheat the oven to 180°C/350°F/Gas Mark 4.

2 Place the rhubarb on a baking tray, sprinkle with the caster sugar and roast in the oven for 12–15 minutes.

3 When cooked, put the rhubarb in a 23-cm/9-inch greased ovenproof dish with the blackberries, vanilla extract and ginger. Stir well to combine.

4 For the topping, rub the margarine and flour together with your fingertips until the mixture resembles fine breadcrumbs. Add the demerara sugar and almonds and mix together. Cover the rhubarb mixture with the crumble topping and bake in the preheated oven for 35–40 minutes until golden. Serve immediately.

8–10 sticks of rhubarb, cut into bite-sized pieces (800 g/1 lb 12 oz total weight)

8 tbsp caster sugar

250 g/9 oz blackberries

½ tsp vanilla extract

½ tsp ground ginger

CRUMBLE TOPPING

100 g/3½ oz vegan and gluten-free margarine, plus extra for greasing

200 g/7 oz gluten-free plain flour

100 g/3½ oz demerara sugar

15 g/½ oz flaked almonds

PREP TIME: 20 minutes COOK TIME: 30–35 minutes SERVES: 8

Pear & Apple OAT CRUMBLE

This makes a great alternative to Christmas pudding for lunch on Christmas Day, with its classic winter-spiced flavours.

- 3 unwaxed cooking apples, peeled, cored and sliced
- 3 unwaxed pears, peeled, cored and sliced
- 3 tsp unwaxed apple juice
- ½ tsp gluten-free cornflour
- ½ tsp ground cinnamon
- 2 tbsp agave syrup
- 2 cloves

OAT CRUMBLE

- 60 g/2¼ oz gluten-free plain flour
- 100 g/3½ oz light soft brown sugar
- 20 g/¾ oz walnuts, chopped
- 60 g/2¼ oz gluten-free porridge oats
- 100 g/3½ oz vegan and gluten-free margarine, plus extra for greasing

1 Preheat the oven to 160°C/325°F/Gas Mark 3. Grease a medium rectangular baking dish.

2 Put the apple, pear, apple juice, cornflour, cinnamon, agave and cloves in a large bowl. Stir well with a wooden spoon to combine.

3 To make the crumble, mix the flour, sugar, walnuts, oats and margarine in a large bowl, rubbing the ingredients together with your fingertips.

4 Spread a small layer of crumble mixture over the base of the prepared baking dish. Arrange the apple and pear mixture on top and sprinkle over the remaining crumble mixture.

5 Bake in the preheated oven for 30–35 minutes until golden brown and crisp on top. Serve immediately.

2

3

4

Cook's tip

This crumble is great with vegan and gluten-free custard or vegan and gluten-free ice cream.

Cook's tip
Ready-made granola is already baked so it doesn't need long in the oven.

PREP TIME: 10 minutes COOK TIME: 25 minutes SERVES: 4–6

Summer Fruit GRANOLA CRUMBLE

This makes a fabulous breakfast or a great summer dessert, with the fresh and fruity flavours combining deliciously with the crunchy granola.

- 200 g/7 oz strawberries
- 200 g/7 oz raspberries
- 200 g/7 oz blueberries
- juice of ½ an unwaxed lemon
- 2 tbsp caster sugar
- 1 tbsp gluten-free cornflour
- 200 g/7 oz vegan and gluten-free granola

1 Preheat the oven to 180°C/350°F/Gas Mark 4.

2 Put the strawberries, raspberries and blueberries into a large mixing bowl. Add the lemon juice, sugar and cornflour and stir to mix the ingredients thoroughly. Transfer the fruit to a deep baking dish that is approximately 15 x 23 cm/6 x 9 inches in size. Bake, uncovered, in the preheated oven for 15 minutes, or until the fruit is softened.

3 Sprinkle the granola over the fruit and bake the dish for a further 10 minutes. Serve immediately.

2

2

3

PREP TIME: 15 minutes COOK TIME: 40 minutes SERVES: 4

Chilli Chocolate SPONGE PUDDINGS

This combination of spicy chilli and decadently rich chocolate is a real winter warmer and makes a great family pudding.

- 70 g/2½ oz vegan and gluten-free margarine, plus extra for greasing
- 50 ml/2 fl oz maple syrup
- 55 g/2 oz gluten-free plain flour
- 3 tbsp vegan and gluten-free cocoa powder
- ½ tsp gluten-free baking powder
- 70 g/2½ oz ground almonds
- pinch of chilli powder

SAUCE

- 225 g/8 oz vegan and gluten-free dark chocolate
- 85 g/3 oz caster sugar
- 125 ml/4 fl oz gluten-free soya cream
- pinch of chilli powder

1 Preheat the oven to 150°C/300°F/Gas Mark 2. Grease four oven-proof ramekins and line with baking paper.

2 Cream the margarine and maple syrup together with a wooden spoon. Add the flour, cocoa powder, baking powder, ground almonds and chilli powder and mix thoroughly. Divide the mixture evenly between the ramekins.

3 Place the ramekins on a small baking tray and bake in the preheated oven for 40 minutes, or until firm and springy to the touch. Leave to cool slightly and then turn out onto serving plates.

4 To make the sauce, break the chocolate into small pieces and place in a small saucepan with the sugar, soya cream and 50 ml/2 fl oz boiling water. Heat gently to melt the chocolate and stir together thoroughly. Add the chilli powder, according to your taste. Pour the sauce over the puddings then serve immediately.

Cook's tip

More subtle spices, such as cinnamon and ground ginger, also work well in this recipe.

2

2

4

Cook's tip
Try adding 2 tablespoons of chopped mixed peel or use almond extract in place of vanilla.

PREP TIME: 15 minutes   COOK TIME: 40 minutes   SERVES: 4

Date & Pistachio PUDDINGS

These are pure comfort food, especially when these individual sponge puddings are served with hot vegan custard on a blustery evening.

1 Preheat the oven to 150°C/300°F/Gas Mark 2. Grease four oven-proof ramekins and line with baking paper.

2 Place the pistachios and dates into a small mixing bowl and mix together with the margarine. Divide the mixture between the ramekins.

3 To make the sponge, cream the margarine and maple syrup together with a wooden spoon. Add the flour, baking powder, ground almonds and vanilla and mix thoroughly. Divide the mixture between the ramekins.

4 Place the ramekins on a small baking tray and bake in the preheated oven for 40 minutes, or until golden and springy to the touch. Turn out onto serving plates and drizzle with warmed maple syrup before serving.

- 70 g/2½ oz vegan and gluten-free margarine, plus extra for greasing
- 50 ml/2 fl oz maple syrup
- 55 g/2 oz gluten-free plain flour
- ½ tsp gluten-free baking powder
- 70 g/2½ oz ground almonds
- ½ tsp vanilla extract
- maple syrup, to serve

TOPPING

- 55 g/2 oz shelled pistachio nuts, finely chopped
- 100 g/3½ oz stoned, unwaxed dates, finely chopped
- 30 g/1 oz vegan and gluten-free margarine

CHAPTER 5

Savoury

PREP TIME: 20 minutes, plus rising

COOK TIME: 40–45 minutes

MAKES: 1 loaf

Seeded Brown BREAD

This is an easy, wholesome loaf, which is best eaten on the day that it is made.

450 g/1 lb gluten-free brown bread flour

½ tsp salt

2 tsp dried yeast

2 tbsp brown sugar

1 tbsp pumpkin seeds

1 tbsp poppy seeds

1 tbsp sunflower seeds

vegan and gluten-free egg replacer, equivalent to 2 eggs

350 ml/12 fl oz gluten-free soya milk, plus extra for brushing

1 tsp vegan and gluten-free cider vinegar

90 ml/3 fl oz rapeseed oil, plus extra for greasing

1 Put the flour, salt, yeast and sugar into a large mixing bowl and stir them together with a wooden spoon. Put the seeds into a small bowl, mix well and set aside 1 tablespoon to be used as the topping.

2 Make up the egg replacer in a small bowl according to the packet instructions and beat it with a fork for a minute until bubbly. In a large measuring jug, mix the soya milk, vinegar, oil and egg replacer together.

3 Add the seeds and wet ingredients to the flour. Mix well with a wooden spoon to form a sticky dough.

4 Place the dough into an oiled 1 kg/2 lb loaf tin and use a spatula to push it into the corners and smooth the top. Cover with oiled clingfilm and leave in a warm place for 1 hour.

5 Preheat the oven to 220°C/425°F/Gas Mark 7.

6 Brush the surface of the loaf with a little soya milk and scatter the reserved seed mixture over the top. Bake in the centre of the preheated oven for 40–45 minutes, or until browned and baked through. Leave to cool in the tin before turning out and slicing.

2

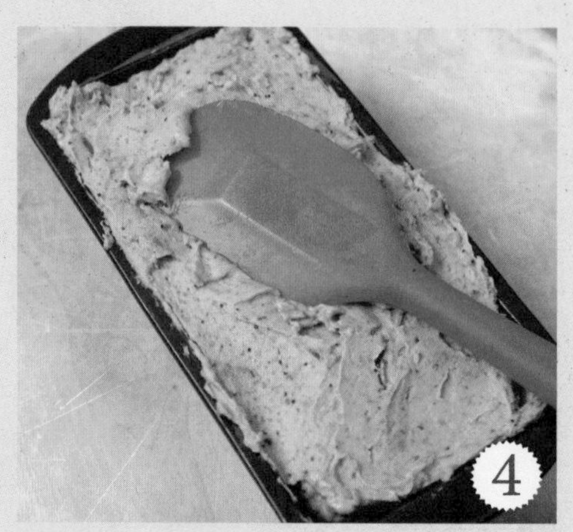
4

6

Cook's tip
The bread does not rise much at step 4, but giving the yeast some time to work does improve the texture and taste of the finished bread loaf.

Cook's tip

You can vary the types of dried fruit included in this recipe to suit your personal tastes.

PREP TIME: 20 minutes, plus standing

COOK TIME: 25-30 minutes

MAKES: 1 loaf

Fruit Soda BREAD

This is a different take on the standard Irish soda bread and is full of dried fruit flavours.

- 55 g/2 oz ready-to-eat stoned unwaxed prunes, chopped
- 55 g/2 oz ready-to-eat dried unwaxed apricots, chopped
- 40 g/1½ oz ready-to-eat dried unwaxed apples, chopped
- 40 g/1½ oz dried cranberries
- 150 ml/5 fl oz unwaxed apple juice
- 450 g/1 lb gluten-free plain flour
- 1½ tbsp gluten-free baking powder
- 2 tsp xanthan gum
- ¼ tsp salt
- 2 tbsp sunflower oil, plus extra for greasing
- 225 ml/8 fl oz gluten-free soya milk, plus extra for brushing
- 4 tbsp maple syrup
- 1 tbsp pumpkin seeds

1 Place the prunes, apricots, apples and cranberries in a bowl and pour over the apple juice. Cover and leave to stand for about 30 minutes.

2 Preheat the oven to 200°C/400°F/Gas Mark 6. Brush a baking tray with oil. Sift the flour, baking powder, xanthan gum and salt into a bowl and make a well in the centre. Mix the oil, milk and maple syrup and add to the well in the dry ingredients with the fruits and juice, mixing lightly to a soft, but not sticky, dough. Add a little more milk if the dough feels dry.

3 Shape the dough to a smooth round on the prepared baking tray, flatten slightly and cut a deep cross through the centre almost to the base. Gently pull the wedges apart at the points. Brush with milk and sprinkle with pumpkin seeds.

4 Bake in the preheated oven for 25–30 minutes, or until golden brown and the base sounds hollow when tapped.

Cook's tip

Experiment with hard vegan and gluten-free cheeses – you may find a blue cheese which works well in this recipe. Soft vegan and gluten-free cheese will make the bread too wet.

PREP TIME: 20 minutes COOK TIME: 45–50 minutes MAKES: 1 loaf

Cheese & Chive BREAD

This soda bread-style loaf uses soya yogurt in place of buttermilk. Try it sliced and toasted with a steaming bowl of soup.

- vegan and gluten-free margarine, for greasing
- 250 g/9 oz gluten-free white bread flour
- 4 tsp gluten-free baking powder
- ½ tsp xanthan gum
- 3 tbsp linseed meal
- vegan and gluten-free egg replacer, equivalent to 3 eggs
- 4 tbsp coconut oil
- 300 ml/10 fl oz gluten-free soya yogurt
- 25 g/1 oz snipped fresh chives
- 125 g/4½ oz vegan and gluten-free cheddar-style cheese, grated

1 Preheat the oven to 180°C/350°F/Gas Mark 4. Grease an 18-cm/7-inch round, springform cake tin and line with baking paper.

2 Sift the flour and baking powder into a large mixing bowl and stir in the xanthan gum and linseed meal with a wooden spoon.

3 Make up the egg replacer in a small bowl according to the packet instructions and beat it with a fork for a minute until bubbly. Add it to the flour mixture, along with the coconut oil and soya yogurt, and stir well to combine.

4 Fold the chives and grated cheese into the mixture and spoon into the prepared tin. Smooth the top with a rubber spatula or leave it rough if you prefer a more rustic look.

5 Bake in the preheated oven for 45–50 minutes, or until a skewer inserted into the centre of the loaf comes out clean. Leave to cool in the tin for 5 minutes, then release the sides of the tin and transfer the bread to a wire rack to cool before slicing.

2

3

4

PREP TIME: 20 minutes, plus standing

COOK TIME: 35–40 minutes

SERVES: 12

Italian Chickpea BREAD

This traditional Italian bread, made with chickpea flour, is perfect for mopping up a rich tomato sauce.

- 250 g/9 oz gram flour
- 4 tbsp extra virgin olive oil
- salt and pepper
- sprigs of fresh rosemary, to garnish

1 Put the flour into a large mixing bowl. Gradually whisk in 850 ml/1½ pints of cold water using a balloon whisk or a hand-held electric whisk. Whisk the mixture until it is completely smooth and then stir in seasoning to taste. Set the bowl aside for 3 hours, to allow the batter to thicken.

2 Preheat the oven to 180°C/350°F/Gas Mark 4.

3 Put the oil into a 33- x 23-cm/13- x 9-inch baking tray with a rim of at least 1 cm/½ inch.

4 Give the batter a quick stir with a wooden spoon and pour it into the baking tray, to form a layer that is approximately 5 mm/¼ inch thick. Arrange the rosemary sprigs in a decorative pattern on top of the batter.

5 Carefully put the baking tray into the preheated oven. A steady hand is useful as the oil underneath the wet batter tends to make it slide about in the tray. Bake for 35–40 minutes, or until golden brown and firm. Allow to cool for 5 minutes in the tray before slicing.

1

4

4

PREP TIME: 15–20 minutes, plus standing

COOK TIME: 1 hour

MAKES: 10

Mexican-style TORTILLA WRAPS

These Mexican flour tortilla wraps can be used for lunchtime wraps or for burrito or fajita dishes.

- 10 g/¼ oz dried yeast
- 400 ml/14 fl oz tepid water
- 2 tbsp sunflower oil
- 400 g/14 oz gluten-free plain flour, plus extra for dusting
- 1½ tsp xanthan gum
- 2 tbsp chopped coriander (optional)
- ½ tsp chilli flakes (optional)
- salt and pepper

1 Mix the yeast, tepid water and oil in a jug and leave at room temperature for approximately 20 minutes until frothy.

2 Sift the flour and xanthan gum into a large bowl and make a well in the centre. Add the yeast liquid to the well slowly with the coriander, chilli, if using, and salt and pepper to taste. Mix well to form a sticky dough.

3 Turn out onto a floured surface and knead well. Divide into 10 small balls.

4 Cut out a circle of baking paper 20 cm/8 inches in diameter and roll out each ball of dough under this, the thinner the better.

5 Place a large frying pan over a medium heat. Add the tortillas to the pan, one at a time, and cook for 2–3 minutes, or until bubbling and turning golden brown. Flip over and cook the other side for 2–3 minutes, or until golden brown. Serve hot or cold with your favourite fillings.

2

4

5

Cook's tip
The chopped, fresh coriander adds an extra dimension to these wraps, but you can also use parsley.

2

3

4

PREP TIME: 15–20 minutes COOK TIME: 25 minutes MAKES: 8

Savoury Potato MUFFINS

These tasty muffins are best eaten straight from the oven and are a great addition to a cooked breakfast.

300 g/10½ oz baked potatoes

vegan and gluten-free egg replacer, equivalent to 2 eggs

150 g/5½ oz vegan and gluten-free margarine, plus extra for greasing

25 g/1 oz brown sugar

175 g/6 oz gluten-free self-raising flour

1 tsp gluten-free baking powder

3 tbsp chopped fresh chives

salt and pepper, to taste

1 Preheat the oven to 180°C/350°F/Gas Mark 4. Grease eight holes of a muffin tin.

2 Scoop the flesh out of the potatoes and mash until smooth. Make up the egg replacer in a small bowl according to the packet instructions and beat it with a fork for a minute until bubbly.

3 Put the margarine and sugar into the bowl of an electric food mixer and cream together. Alternatively, put the margarine and sugar into a large mixing bowl and cream together with a hand-held electric mixer or a fork. Then add all the remaining ingredients and continue to mix until all the ingredients are just combined. Over-mixing can make the potato sticky so just make sure that the egg replacer and chives are well distributed.

4 Divide the mixture between the prepared holes of the muffin tin and bake in the preheated oven for 25 minutes, or until crisp and golden.

Cook's tip

Leftover baked potatoes work well in this recipe, but you can use freshly boiled potatoes too. You just need to make sure the potatoes are as dry as possible.

PREP TIME: 20 minutes COOK TIME: 25 minutes MAKES: 12

Beetroot MUFFINS

These unusual sweet-savoury muffins are best served warm, spread with dairy-free butter or coconut oil.

- 225 g/8 oz gluten-free plain flour
- 1½ tsp gluten-free baking powder
- 1½ tsp gluten-free bicarbonate of soda
- ½ tsp xanthan gum
- 1 tsp salt
- 1 tsp ground cinnamon
- 1 tsp ground ginger
- 75 ml/2½ fl oz coconut oil
- 100 ml/3½ fl oz agave nectar
- 150 ml/5 fl oz gluten-free soya milk
- 115 g/4 oz raw beetroot, trimmed, peeled and grated

1 Preheat the oven to 180°C/350°F/Gas Mark 4. Line a 12-hole muffin tin with paper cases.

2 Put the flour, baking powder, bicarbonate of soda, xanthan gum, salt, cinnamon and ginger into a large mixing bowl and stir together with a wooden spoon. Add the oil, agave nectar and soya milk and mix well. Add the beetroot and stir until well combined.

3 Divide the mixture equally between the muffin cases.

4 Bake in the preheated oven for 25 minutes, or until a skewer inserted into the centre of a muffin comes out clean. Leave to cool in the tin for 5 minutes before turning out onto a wire rack to cool.

Cook's tip

Agave nectar adds sweetness without affecting the taste of the muffins. Coconut oil may be solid at cooler temperatures – if you need to melt it, let it cool before adding it to the mixture to stop the baking powder acting too quickly.

PREP TIME: 20 minutes COOK TIME: 20–25 minutes MAKES: 12

Jalapeño Cornmeal MUFFINS

These savoury muffins are best served warm, and are good with a hearty soup or vegan chilli.

1 Preheat the oven to 180°C/350°F/Gas Mark 4. Grease a 12-hole muffin tin.

2 Mix the soya milk and cider vinegar together in a large jug and set aside to curdle.

3 Put the cornmeal, baking powder, bicarbonate of soda and salt into a large mixing bowl and stir together with a wooden spoon.

4 Pour the curdled soya milk over the cornmeal mixture, add the apple sauce, maple syrup, olive oil and jalapeño, and quickly stir the mixture together. Divide the mixture equally between the greased holes in the muffin tin and bake in the preheated oven for 20–25 minutes, or until a skewer inserted into the centre of a muffin comes out clean. Leave to cool in the tin for 5 minutes, then turn out and serve warm.

vegan and gluten-free margarine, for greasing

250 ml/9 fl oz gluten-free soya milk

1 tbsp vegan and gluten-free cider vinegar

300 g/10½ oz fine cornmeal

1 tbsp gluten-free baking powder

1 tsp gluten-free bicarbonate of soda

1 tsp salt

4 tbsp gluten-free, unwaxed apple sauce

3 tbsp maple syrup

4 tbsp olive oil

1 unwaxed jalapeño pepper, deseeded and chopped

PREP TIME: 15 minutes   COOK TIME: 15–20 minutes   MAKES: 8

Herby SCONES

These scones are best served hot, straight from the oven with dairy-free butter or freshly roasted garlic cloves.

- 250 g/9 oz gluten-free plain flour
- 60 g/2¼ oz vegan and gluten-free margarine, plus extra for greasing
- 4 tsp gluten-free baking powder
- 2 tbsp finely chopped fresh herbs, such as thyme and sage
- 2 tbsp nutritional yeast flakes
- pepper, to taste
- 175 ml/6 fl oz gluten-free soya milk
- 1 tbsp poppy seeds

1 Preheat the oven to 200°C/400°F/Gas Mark 6. Grease a large baking sheet.

2 Put the flour into a large mixing bowl. Rub in the margarine using your fingertips until the texture is like soft breadcrumbs. Stir in the baking powder, herbs, yeast flakes and pepper. Add the soya milk and stir the mixture with a wooden spoon to make a soft, sticky dough.

3 Turn the mixture out onto the greased baking sheet and use a palette knife or rubber spatula to shape it into a round. Use a sharp knife to mark it into eight sections and sprinkle the poppy seeds over the top.

4 Bake in the preheated oven for 15–20 minutes, or until cooked through and a skewer inserted into the loaf comes out clean. Leave to cool on the sheet for 5 minutes, then cut into sections and serve warm.

Cook's tip
You can use a mixture of fresh herbs or choose one of your favourites instead – sage, rosemary and chives all work well.

2

3

4

PREP TIME: 20 minutes | COOK TIME: 40–45 minutes | MAKES: 4

Roast Pepper CROSTATAS

These adaptable individual tarts are great for lunch at your desk or a picnic.

- a mix of 5 unwaxed red, yellow or orange peppers, deseeded and sliced
- 2 tbsp sunflower oil

DOUGH

- 250 g/9 oz gluten-free self-raising flour, plus extra for dusting
- 2 tbsp nutritional yeast flakes
- pinch of salt
- 55 g/2 oz vegan and gluten-free margarine
- 150 ml/5 fl oz gluten-free soya milk

1 Preheat the oven to 190°C/375°F/Gas Mark 5.

2 Spread the pepper slices out in a baking dish and drizzle with the oil. Bake in the preheated oven for 15–20 minutes, or until softened but not browning. Set aside to cool and leave the oven on.

3 To make the dough, put the flour, yeast flakes and salt into a large mixing bowl and stir with a wooden spoon to combine. Rub in the margarine with your fingertips, then gradually stir in the milk and use your hands to bring the mixture together as a soft dough.

4 Transfer the dough to a lightly floured board and knead it gently to form a smooth ball. Cut the dough into four equal pieces and roll each piece out to line and slightly overhang four 12-cm/4½-inch round, loose-based individual flan tins. Don't trim away the excess pastry!

5 Divide the roast peppers between the four tins and gently fold the pastry up over the filling.

6 Bake in the preheated oven for 20–25 minutes, or until golden. Serve hot or cold.

Cook's tip

You could add vegan and gluten-free cheese to this dish – if you use a meltable type, put it on top of the peppers before folding up the pastry. If it's not meltable, cut into small cubes and mix with the roasted peppers before you fill the crostatas.

PREP TIME: 20 minutes, plus rising

COOK TIME: 15 minutes

MAKES: 20

Seeded BREADSTICKS

Nutritional yeast flakes give a cheesy flavour to these versatile crunchy breadsticks.

- vegan and gluten-free egg replacer, equivalent to 2 eggs
- 350 g/12 oz gluten-free white bread flour, plus extra for dusting
- 2 tsp xanthan gum
- 2 tsp caster sugar
- 3 tbsp nutritional yeast flakes
- 2 tbsp olive oil
- 1 tbsp pepper
- 7 g/¼ oz dried yeast
- vegetable oil, for greasing
- 1 tbsp white sesame seeds
- 1 tbsp black sesame seeds

1 Make up the egg replacer in a small bowl according to the packet instructions and beat it with a fork for a minute until bubbly. Divide the egg mixture into two equal portions. Set one portion aside to glaze the breadsticks with later.

2 If you have a breadmaker, load it with the flour, xanthan gum, caster sugar, yeast flakes, olive oil, one portion of the egg replacer and the pepper. Sprinkle the dried yeast on top and add 225 ml/8 fl oz of warm water (not too hot, as this will kill the yeast). Set the machine to a 'dough' setting and start.

3 If you don't have a breadmaker, sift the flour and xanthan gum into a large mixing bowl. Add the dried yeast, yeast flakes, sugar and pepper, and mix together with a wooden spoon. Use the spoon to make a 'well' in the centre of the bowl. Mix the olive oil and one portion of the egg replacer together with 225 ml/8 fl oz of warm water in a large jug. Pour this wet mixture into the well in the dry ingredients and use a wooden spoon to stir all the ingredients together. Dust a large chopping board with flour, turn the dough out onto the board and knead it for 5 minutes until it forms a smooth ball. Put the dough into a large bowl, cover with greased clingfilm and leave in a warm place to rise for about an hour, or until doubled in size.

4 Preheat the oven to 220°C/425°F/Gas Mark 7. Grease a large baking sheet and line with baking paper.

5 Dust a large chopping board with flour and turn the dough out onto the board. Pat it into a large sausage shape and cut into 20 equal pieces. Gently roll each piece into a long thin stick, about 30 cm/12 inches long, and transfer the breadsticks to the prepared sheet. Brush each stick with the reserved egg replacer and then sprinkle them with the black and white sesame seeds.

6 Bake in the preheated oven for 15 minutes, or until just golden. Allow to cool a little before transferring to a wire rack to crisp up.

Cook's tip

Make sure there are no lumps in your egg replacer mixture – these can leave some unsightly white marks when glazing your breadsticks.

PREP TIME: 20 minutes, plus rising

COOK TIME: 15 minutes

MAKES: 20

Rosemary & Garlic BREADSTICKS

These breadsticks are tasty enough to be served on their own, without any dips. Serve with Italian food or offer them as a snack with drinks.

- vegan and gluten-free egg replacer, equivalent to 2 eggs
- 350 g/12 oz gluten-free white bread flour, plus extra for dusting
- 2 tsp xanthan gum
- 2 tsp caster sugar
- 2 tbsp olive oil
- 7 g/¼ oz dried yeast
- vegetable oil, for greasing
- 2 tbsp finely chopped fresh rosemary
- 1 tbsp garlic powder

1 Make up the egg replacer in a small bowl according to the packet instructions and beat it with a fork for a minute until bubbly. Divide the egg mixture into two equal portions. Set one portion aside to glaze the breadsticks with later.

2 If you have a breadmaker, load it with the flour, xanthan gum, caster sugar, olive oil and one portion of the egg replacer. Sprinkle the dried yeast on top and add 225 ml/8 fl oz of warm water (not too hot, as this will kill the yeast). Set the machine to a 'dough' setting and start.

3 If you don't have a breadmaker, sift the flour and xanthan gum into a large mixing bowl. Add the dried yeast and sugar, and mix together with a wooden spoon. Use the spoon to make a 'well' in the centre of the bowl. Mix the olive oil and one portion of the egg replacer together with 225 ml/8 fl oz of warm water in a large jug. Pour this wet mixture into the well in the dry ingredients and use a wooden spoon to stir all the ingredients together. Dust a large chopping board with flour, turn the dough out onto the board and knead it for 5 minutes until it forms a smooth ball. Put the dough into a large bowl, cover with greased clingfilm and leave in a warm place to rise for about an hour, or until doubled in size.

4 Preheat the oven to 220°C/425°F/Gas Mark 7. Grease a large baking sheet and line with baking paper.

5 Dust a large chopping board with flour. Sprinkle the rosemary and garlic powder over the flour. Turn the dough out onto the board and knead it until the rosemary and garlic powder are well incorporated into the dough. Pat it into a large sausage shape and cut into 20 equal pieces. Gently roll each piece into a long thin stick, about 30 cm/12 inches long, and transfer the breadsticks to the prepared sheet. Brush each stick with the reserved egg replacer.

6 Bake in the preheated oven for 15 minutes, or until just golden. Allow to cool a little before transferring to a wire rack to crisp up.

Cook's tip

If you want to try using other herbs, it's always best to use dried rather than fresh herbs so you can avoid adding any unwanted moisture to the dough.

2

5

5

Cook's tip

Rolling your dough thinly will create crisp crackers, but take care not to burn them – check underneath as the bases will brown more quickly than the tops.

PREP TIME: 15 minutes COOK TIME: 15–18 minutes MAKES: 30

Cracker BITES

These crispy little crackers make a guilt-free snack – use a selection of small cookie cutters to make a variety of pretty shapes.

175 g/6 oz gluten-free plain flour, plus extra for dusting
30 g/1 oz nutritional yeast flakes
1 tsp dried thyme
3 tbsp rapeseed oil
salt and pepper

1 Preheat the oven to 180°C/350°F/Gas Mark 4. Cover a large baking sheet with baking paper.

2 Put the flour, yeast flakes and thyme into a large mixing bowl and season to taste. Stir the mixture with a wooden spoon to combine.

3 Stir in the oil and gradually add 6–7 tablespoons of cold water. Use your hands to bring the mixture together to form a dough that is soft but not sticky.

4 Turn the dough out onto a lightly floured board and roll it to around 3 mm/⅛ inch thick. Use a small cookie cutter (2.5–5 cm/1–2 inches in diameter) to cut out the crackers and place them on the prepared baking sheet. Re-roll the dough trimmings and make as many crackers as you can.

5 Bake in the preheated oven for 15–18 minutes, or until just golden on the bottom. Leave the crackers to cool on the baking sheet for a few minutes, then use a palette knife to transfer them to a wire rack to cool.

Index